Nano Reef

Bonsai Style Hand Book

Jimmie Wayne Piersall

iUniverse books may be ordered through booksellers or by contacting:

iUniverse
1663 Liberty Drive
Bloomington, IN 47403
www.iuniverse.com
1-800-Authors (1-800-288-4677)

Because of the dynamic nature of the Internet, any web addresses or links contained in this book may have changed since publication and may no longer be valid. The views expressed in this work are solely those of the author and do not necessarily reflect the views of the publisher, and the publisher hereby disclaims any responsibility for them.

Any people depicted in stock imagery provided by Getty Images are models, and such images are being used for illustrative purposes only.
Certain stock imagery © Getty Images.

ISBN: 978-1-5320-4825-8 (sc)
ISBN: 978-1-5320-4826-5 (e)

Library of Congress Control Number: 2018904851

Print information available on the last page.

iUniverse rev. date: 05/18/2018

If you're anything like me, you find marine life fascinating! When I was a young boy, growing up in Southern California, I always loved my family trips to the beach. While everyone was swimming in the waves, I would be in the rocky areas looking for marine animals. I would find many and take some home. I always loved the idea of keeping a saltwater aquarium. A few more years went by and I eventually ordered dwarf seahorses from the back of a magazine. I remember opening the box and seeing them for the first time, those tiny little ponies. I fell in love right then; I knew I was hooked! Years later I moved to Florida and remembered where my tiny sea ponies were from, so I began my search. Almost daily I dragged my net across the sea floor through the sea grass beds. I would catch all kinds of marine life; stingrays, sole fish, gobies, blennies, pufferfish, boxfish, nudibranch, sea hares, pipefish, hermit crabs, decorator crabs, tons of shrimp, amphapods and, finally my seahorses (hippocampus zosterae) and their large relative, the lines seahorse (hippocampus erectus). I knew from this moment on this is what I wanted to do with the rest of my life! After I began my studies of marine life, I wrote this book so I hope you enjoy it as much as I have, into the mini sea as we go!

To start with, water us key. The world is 71% covered by water, the sea is a vast expanse filled with mystery and unusual creatures, some have yet to be discovered. There are canyons and trenches larger and deeper than the Grand Canyon. The tropics in and around the equator, the tropic of cancer, and the tropic of Capricorn, are covered with corals. There are many temperate water corals as well as many species that are non-photo synthesizing. They are only plankton eaters thereby are others that grow what is called coralline algae in their tissue, this feeds them for the most part although they eat plankton as well. Did you know that Alaska's Aleutian Islands Chain may harbor the greatest abundance of temperate water corals in the world?! So with patience and time, you can perfect your reef keeping skills and be able to keep your own little world.

Chapter 1   Water Quality

Your mini reef's water quality is key to be successful and if you stay as close to these perimeters as possible, you should be successful and have a balanced ecosystem!

The Bonsai Concept

This concept is everything in a miniature form, the rocks that look like mountains and trees that look old and wise. Your coral reef can be trimmed and kept small. Your equipment can all be placed in a sump filter unseen and you can go for a more natural look. You can have a micro train set or a tidal beach with waves breaking over a multi colored zoanthids. Corals and maybe a shrimp gobie and pistol shrimp because they look like little lobsters. Mountain, waterfalls, and Zen sand gardens on flat mounts above the water's surface with marble spheres. The key is to think small.

Water Parameters

It will take 6 to 8 weeks for your nano tank to cycle. This can be done with a hardy fish like a molly (Poecilia sp.) or you can add a small amount of fish food, this will raise the ammonia and increase the beneficial nitrating bacteria. Either way works fine and all throughout this cycle you should test your water quality and remember to add your corals last!

The Nitrogen Cycle

1. Your fish produce waste into ammonia.
2. Your ammonia levels rise.
3. The nitrating bacteria rise.
4. The bacteria convert ammonia into nitrites and are deadly to marine life.
5. The beneficial bacteria increase in numbers and nitrites are converted to nitrates and these are acceptable at lower levels.

Water Changes

Water changes are important because they replace lost micro nutrions and trace elements. They also remove waste or proteins and replace water loss through evaporation. Water changes on a regular basis will benefit your nano reef!

PH and Alkalinity

The PH and alkalinity levels should be maintained around 7.9 to 8.2 in your calcium, calcium carbonate and magnesium levels are maintained. The PH and alkalinity or water hardness should maintain itself, but a monthly testing will do.

Calcium

Calcium is one of the most important elements in stony coral's growth and development! This should be maintained around 400 ppm to 450 ppm although 500 ppm would not be harmful. Stony corals and giant clams would deplete these levels in rapid succession so saying this it is recommended that you test your calcium levels at least once a week. A drip eclameter will be beneficial at maintaining the desired levels. Calcium is also beneficial for other invertebrates like crabs, and shrimp. This aids in development of their exoskeleton and in the deep blue sea calcium helps build the nautilus beautiful shell!

Magnesium

Magnesium is also an important part of stony corals skeleton growth and development and should be maintained around 1100 to 1300 ppm. Magnesium acts as a buffering agent and helps maintain your PH and alkalinity. Magnesium also aids in preventing calcium from bonding to carbonates making it unusable and depletes carbonates and waste calcium and may reduce alkalinity. Magnesium should be tested at least once a week.

Strontium

Strontium is a calcium based element and helps coral's tissue adhere to the skeleton more readily and should be maintained at 7.0 ppm to 10.0 ppm. Use caution, don't overdose strontium, it can be toxic!

Iodine

Iodine is little more than a trace element and should be maintained at 0.5 ppm to 0.8 ppm. Iodine is beneficial to many marine flora and fana and this includes some types of macro alleges, corals, crustaceans, and fish. Iodine acts as a detoxifying agent by bonding with oxygen molecules and changes into iodate which reduces irritation in marine life tissue. This is why iodine is added to you nano reef tank. Use caution, don't overdose, this may destroy beneficial bacteria.

Trace Elements

Trace elements make up less than 0.0005% in seawater, however corals seem to benefit by trace elements. Mud filters are a great way to maintain trace elements and are highly recommended. Regular water changes will also help replace trace elements.

Phosphate

Phosphate can be a nano reef's worse nightmare. They can cause massive cyanobacteria and algae blooms. The main cause for these outbreaks are carbon chips. Always use phosphate free carbon chips and over feeding and decaying fish foods and excessive waste. Remember you must feed in accordance to your nano reef's size! Regular water changes will help reduce phosphate. A UV sterilizer is beneficial and phosphate absorbing pads are most effective.

Silica

Silica is a mineral that can cause diatom bloom outbreaks! One way to keep silica out of nano reef is to use R.O. water. There are some filter material that can keep your reef tank clear of diatoms. Your aquarium's glass also contains silica and silicon but this usually has little effect on your nano tank. Keep it simple, use R.O. water.

Chapter 2   Equipment

Choosing your equipment is important but that does not mean there are not ways of setting up your nano reef tank that can be cost effective or down right fun to build yourself! There is equipment that you have to buy but there is equipment you don't! The choice is yours on how creative you want to be. I'm a D.I.Y. guy myself!

The Nano Reef Tank

Nanos are easy to build if you want to keep it simple, but I like a challenge! The size, shape, height, and length are up to you. Glass or plexi-glass work well but plexi-glass scratches easily but is stronger than glass and easier to drill and glass is scratch resistant. Silicon sealant works well with either but plexi-glass may require a little more. You can also build your own sump, protein skimmer, sand filter, phosphate reactor, U.V. sterilizer and more! If you don't want to cut or drill your own nano tank, most glass shops can do this for you. Cylinder nano tanks may need a specialty glass shop.

The Sump

It's my opinion that a sump is pivotal for a nano tank. You are dealing with a very confined space and a sump increases space and more room to work with and also increases water valium. The sump gives a more natural look with no unsitly equipment in view.

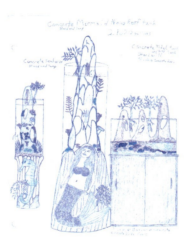

A Compartmentlisted Nano Tank

There is nothing wrong with compartmentisting your nano reef tank but this does leave less room or space for equipment that may be seen and looks less natural. However, they do work well.

Lighting

Lighting a nano reef tank is far less costly than a larger tank. T5's or Power Compact Florescent Lighting works well. I recommend at least 10 watts per gallon for most soft corals and some LPS corals and 20 watts per gallon for most sps, lps, Corals and Giant Clams. L.E.D. lights or Light Emitting Diodes go by lumens per watt so you can base this on your lighting needs for whatever marine flora and fana you are keeping. L.E.D.s are much more efficient and run cooler and overall are better choice and rember light lovers to the top of the reef!

Lighting and Kelvin Temperature

Kelvin temperatures are light changes as you go deeper in the water you lose, yellows, reds, and whites. Then mostly blues are what's left. For instance, full spectrum range is 5000k to 7500k. More reds, yellows and whites and more blues as you go deeper into the water. Most photosynthesizing corals grow in the 7500k to 20.000 Kelvin temperature range. Photosynthesizing corals grow what is called Zooanthilia also known as Coralline Algae in their tissue or flesh and these produce sugar starch enzymes that feed the corals and most of their food or energy is produced this way. This is why Kelvin temperatures are so important.

Temperatures and Heating

Temperatures on the reef tend to fluctuate some throughout the year. Hurricanes, rain storms, may affect the water chemistry and perhaps ebbing and pulling of the tides do to the magnetic flections of the moon and moon fazes. This is the reason why corals know when to spawn. This usually happens during the New Moon in late Fall or early Winter. The temperature is still important and it's my opinion that corals will thrive better on the somewhat cooler side around 70 to 76 degrees is ideal. Temperature above 82 degrees will cause your corals to push out their zooanthila or Coralline algae and they may not recover. This is known as coral bleaching and has caused massive die off in the wild!

Heating

If you do use a heater for your nano reef tank, this should be a small 25 watts or less for up to a 20 gallon nano tank. Anything more is excessive unless your house is made of ice cubes. I think your nano tank will be fine, your fish and corals are far more likely to check out from overheating than from being too cool! If you're comfortable in the same room, then your nano reef tank is too.

The Protein Skimmer

The protein skimmer in an important tool and may be the most important. They can strip the water of proteins or waste in a short amount of time, but can also strip the water of calcium, magnesium and other minerals as well. This is where water changes and a drip eclameter come in handy. You can buy or make your own protein skimmer. The Venteri skimmers are one of the better kinds.

The Drip Eclameter

The drip eclameter is an essential tool to have over your sump. They can be useful to replace evaporated water or adding calcium, magnesium or other essential minerals. The drip eclameter can be made with a rodent water bottle with a plastic or rubber end or lid, but no metal. The nosal can be replaced with an airline tube with a check valve set to the desired drip. You can also make a drip eclameter out of plexi-glass.

U.V. Sterilizer

The U.V. sterilizer is a good way to keep algae like didoms and marine pathogens out of the nano reef like cryptocaryon irritans. They also help keep your water crystal clear and you can buy a U.V. sterilizer or you can make one yourself. You can buy quartz sleeves or you can make a sleeve out of thin plexi-glass and these need to be covered. Lighting from a U.V. light can affect your eyes. Water needs to run slowly across the U.V. light for maximum exposure in order to reduce a didom and pathogens.

Easy Fri Transfer

Another option is to connect the Kreisel fri tank to the main nano tank for safe and easy fri transfer. This can be done with an inflow pipe and an outflow pipe. The inflow pipe can be connected or placed near the top of the nano with a small LED light run at the end of the outflow. During the night when the fish eggs hatch the fri will be drawn to the LED light and be sucked down the inflow pipe to the kreisel tank safely with decreased losses of fri. The outflow pipe can be run back into the sump or the main tank with a smaller pump and into the Kreisel tank. The outflow can be micro screened off to keep the fri in the kreisel tank.

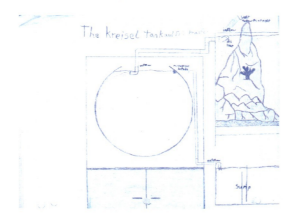

The Kreisel Tank

The Kreisel tanks are very beneficial for fry larva and shrimp larva and have proven to increase their survival rates. These circular tanks help keep the fry suspended and away from the sides and in the mild current with there foods. These tanks have also proven beneficial for jellyfish. The Kreisel tank was built for jellyfish. This is how to build your own kreisel tank.

1. Take a thin piece of acrylic sheet of plexi-glass ¼ inch.
2. Take two sheets of ¼ inch thick for the front and back.
3. You will need to roll the acrylic sheet up and tie with fishing line or string in order to hold the sheet in a roll position.
4. Now you will need to put the rolled and tied acrylic sheet in the over on low about 140 to 160 degrees for about 10 minutes. You need to watch this the entire time to make sure it doesn't melt.
5. After it cools, cut the ties and bend and place between the 2 flat sheets and silicone the bent sheet of acrylic to the flat sheets and let set for 24 hours, and your good to go.

Another way is to cut small sheets like hexagon pattern and silicone one piece at a time two flat glass or plexi-glass sheets front and back. Then start with the bottom piece and work your way up.

Tidial Touch Tank

This is a great way to get people and children interested in marine life. These nanos can have a lower profile and wider tank. These nanos can have all sorts of marine life including corals, macro algae, fish, crabs, snails, sea urchins, starfish and sea anenomies. How do you make your tank tidial? First, you need a digital timer. This can turn pumps on or off throughout the day or night. Now some pumps can make waves by shutting them on or off rapidly or you can buy a wave maker controller, this is easier. Then you will need your sump to be larger or deeper than your nano tidal touch tank. This will hold more water when your main pumps are off. The outflow pipe should be at the desired water level is at its lowest and the outflow pipe should have a shut off valve that's left partially open flowing slowly into the sump. The water will drain in the main tank and some corals and macro algae will be exposed and can remain exposed for about an hour without harm. The main pump is turned back on with the timer and the nano tank fills up to the top overflow drain pipe and this is how a Tidial Touch Tank is made. This is where making your own live rock comes in handy. You can create mini mountains with waterfalls or rocks in and around the tank. This makes a interesting display. Anything you can think of, the choice is yours!

Concrete Stands

Concrete stands can be made out of wood forms. You can mold shapes like hexagons, squares, triangles, or even circles. You can make statues with sumps built into them, these statues can be made from plaster forms and then out of concrete.

Mirror Glass Stands

Mirror glass stands can be made of wood and/or thick plexi-glass covered with cut to form mirror glass and the back and sides of nano tank can be covered with mirror glass and you can even make the front of the stand a clock with a clock kit and chime.

Nano Reef Clocks

Clocks on the front of the stand are also a cool idea and maybe even chimes. You can buy clock making kits at most hobby stores.

Weather Chimes

Weather chimes or music. These are nice for tidal reef tanks or wave making machines like the sounds of; rain, waves, thunder (if you have lightning settings on your LED lights), with a rain system, these can look and sound cool.

A Rain System

Rain makers are possible but you will need a pump on a timer and a rain bar or two. This can be a 1/2 inch pvc pipe with a cap on one end with holes drilled into it and a elbow and 1/2 inch pipe running into the pump.

Under Waterfall

This is a cool idea, these pull the water through a pipe and elbow with a bubbler and this pulls the bubble downwards across the rocks and back through the pipe.

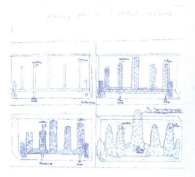

The Gravity Sphere

This can be created with a small sphere or globe. The sphere sits above the water on rock work with an open bottom and is filled all the way with water and with food pumped into it with a baster. Fish will swim up in and above the water line. This creates a cool affect and if fish are fed on a regular basis in the sphere, they will swim in and out on their own. This is a great idea for separating dotty back females from the male. Make the entrance big enough for the female only to enter.

Making Your Own Live Rock

Making your own live rock is a fun and easy project. First off, you will need a few things.

1. A 1/2 inch pvc plastic pipe cut and connect your pipe with T's and elbows. This will create your frame and can be filled with sand for stability.
2. You will need a plastic mesh or rabbit fencing. This looks similar to chicken wire. Cut down to desired shape and tie the ends with plastic zip ties or fishing string line. Then place the mesh over your pvc pipe frame and intake and out flow pipes.
3. You will also need non-toxic pond foam. Spray this around the pvc mesh frame just inside the mesh. If this puffs up too much, it can be easily cut back to form after the foam dries.
4. You will also need a ready concrete mix and color sand, small shells can be added to the mix and rock salt for a natural look. This makes the live rock more porous. Mix on the dry side and then add to your foam frame plus the intake, out flow pipes to your desired look. You may need to soak this frame for up to 6 to 8 weeks. This is due to the increased calcium and alkalinity levels as they are excessive at this time. You can do this cycling during the nitrogen cycle. The rocks will cure and with lots of water, changes in 2 to 6 months, your rocks will come alive with micro fana.

Making a Live Rock Feeder Bowl Shell

You can make a feeder bowl separate or into the Live rock frame. This is made the same way as the live rock but with a open ended pvc pipe top and bottom with a shell bowl at the bottom integrated into the live rock. The food is dropped through the pipe and down into the bowl below. This is designed for finicky eaters like Seahorses and other difficult species. The bowl helps to switch over to frozen foods and fish will associate the feeder bowl as a feeding station.

Viewing Caves and Tunnels

These caves and tunnels are made from homemade live rock and are a great way to view your more secretive marine life like pistol shrimp, gobies and scorpion fish. These viewing caves and tunnels give us a deeper understanding of marine life.

Fragging Corals

Most corals reproduce asexually. This is called budding or branching new coral polyps and these can be cut or fragged into new coral colonies. For soft corals, a razor blade or a pair of scissors will work and these can be put in a tray of small rocks and the corals will attach themselves to these rocks and these rocks can be attached to a plug with superglue. Now lps and sps corals, you can cut or clip with bone cutters or you can use an electric saw and the coral frags can be attached to a plug with superglue. The best way to prevent infection is to use Potassium iodine and Vitamin C for a more rapid recovery. A frag grow out tank is best and are easy to build. They do not need to be very large and can still grow a lot of frags. Gorgonians fragging must be done under the water to prevent tissue die off.

Foggers

Foggers create a beautiful mist that can float above and across the water's surface. You can integrate an outflow pvc pipe through your rock work and the fog will flow. The fog can replace evaporated water loss. Foggers create a natural affect in the nano reef tank.

Filter Media and Material

Carbon: Carbon is a good filter material in that it can help keep the water clean and helps reduce any odors. Use Phosphate free carbon, this will reduce cyanobacteria and algae blooms.

Alternatives to Carbon: Resin beads that absorb organic compounds, these types of media are usually Phosphate free.

Phosphate Removing Media: Phosphate pads or beads work well at obsorbing phosphates and reduce cyanobacteria and algae blooms. Add a little at a time, rapid falls in phosphates can be harmful.

BioBalls: Bioballs work well as a filter material in your sump. Over time they build up beneficial bacteria. They can build up waste material as well and may need to be flushed out on occasion.

Live Rock: Live Rock is a great way to stabilize your nano tank quick! These rocks are very porous and filled with beneficial bacteria, macro algae and sponges and other beneficial marine life. The down side is there are pest species as well like; bristle worm, mantis shrimp and hydroids and more. Hydroids are harmful to dwarf seahorses, Live Rock is not recommended for them! Dry Limestone is safer and will come to life overtime. I recommend that you flush out your Live Rock from time to time. Small pieces work well in a sump as filtration.

Live Sand Filter: The Live Sand Filter is a great way to filter your nano reef and very affective. Sand filters are full of beneficial bacteria and one of the better filtration methods. How to make a live sand filter. One way is to place a pvc pipe in the back of a sandpit and pump the sand. The second is to make a chamber with an open ended V. Run the pvc pipe up the open end of the V and your sand blasting!

Algae turf Filters for Your Sump: Algae filters are a great way to remove waste and help reduce nitrates. You can easily make your own. One way is to use a piece of plexi-glass, cut the center out and place netting screen and then fiberglass screen, silicone the two pieces of plexi-glass over the screens. Place your Algae filter close to the top of the water under full spectrum light 7500k and the algae will start to grow. Scrape most of this off periodically but you should leave some so that it will regrow faster, this will remove excessive amounts of nitrates. These are very efficient filters.

Macro Algae Filters: Macro algae can be grown in the tank or sump or both! The macro algae grows rapidly and help reduce nitrates. You can trim them back and this removal also aids in reducing nitrates. Macro algae can reduce the Ph at night. It's my experience that this seems to have little effect on marine organisms including corals. Red Macro Algae also seems to give off a pleasant sea smell odor.

Mineral Mud: Mud in the nano or sump. Mud nourishes corals and macro algae and replace lost trace elements and helps with filtration. Mud is filled with benifal bacteria. You will notice a positive response from corals, their palps will be more responsive. These muds seem to have a positive response to amphipods and copepods population as well. Booster replacements are available when marine life seems less responsive.

Chapter 3 Disease's Life Cycles Symptoms

Marine fish diseases can easily be prevented with healthy stock. Here are a few things to look out for torn or clasped fins, rapid breathing, popped out eye or eyes, sunken bodies or red lesions, scratching objects is a sign of external parasites, shimming or jerking movement is a sign of dropsy often with clasped fins usually do increase nitrates, fussy or raised areas on the body or specks on the fish. These are signs of illness, use caution, buy only healthy stock and maintain water quality. This will reduce problems.

Quarantine/Hospital Tanks

Quarantine or hospital tanks are the most effective way next to buying good stock of preventing unwanted introduction of disease! Illness can lead to an entire breakdown of your tank. I also recommend that coral and live rock are quarantined in order to prevent unwanted pests or disease. U.V. Sterilizers are highly recommended for a quarantine/hospital tank and remember to leave the charcoal out of the hospital tank because it absorbs medicines.

Fresh Water dips

Fresh water dips are a great way of removing many parasites. The osmotic pressure can cause some parasites to burst corals with brown jelly or some other ailments. A fresh water dip can help reduce parasites. Coral's and sensitive fish species, the Ph and temperature should be the same, about 2-5 minutes, a little longer for hardy species of fish.

Marine Velvet Disease (Amyloodinium Ocellatum)

These dinoflagellate algae area protozoan and they have three life cycles.

Stage 1- The trophonts attached to the fish to feed.
Stage 2- Encysted tomont is the reproductive stage, they divide on the fish.
Stage 3- The dinospores is a free swimming new parasite looking for a new fish host.

Symptoms of disease; rapid breathing (the gills are usually attacked first), clouded fins and eyes skin until they look like salt grains, yellowish in color and more velvety in extreme cases, usually incurable at this point.

Marine Ich (Cryptocaryon Irritans)

This is one of the most common diseases you may encounter. Marine ichs life cycles can last a month or more and has three life cycles.

> Stage 1- "Trophont" will feed under the skin or gills of fish.
> Stage 2- "Tomant" will disattach from the fish host and form a cyst for reproduction.
> Stage 3- "Tomite" cyst opens three days to a month later to release many new parasites ready and searching for a new host.

Symptoms include; white specks, a few at first and then many and can affect breathing or even damage the gills or specks over the eyes and fins!

Brooklynella hostilis

B. hostilla is a ciliated protozoan and can kill with rapid succession and is very contagious. These parasites reproduce by mytosis on a fish host. Direct contact with infected fish can cause outbreaks. Quarantine is recommended. The host fish's skin and blood provide food for B. hostillis and often cause damage. Symptoms; rapid breathing, white specks on the surface of the host fish.

Uronema marinum

This ectoparasite is a ciliate and are often present in waste and decaying matter. Outbreaks caused by high nitrates which can stress. Symptoms; red ringed lesions, excessive slime and missing scales.

Fungal Infections and Bacteria

Fin rot is a bacterial infection caused do to increased nitrate in which causes stress. The bacterial fungus will attack open or infected areas. The following are a list of these attackers; Pseudomonas sp, aeromonas sp, edwaredsiella sp, vibrio sp, cytaphaga sp. These fungal bacterias usually followed by secondary infestation of parasites.

Coral Health

Coral bleaching can occur in the home aquarum, this is often caused by increased temperatures. There's little cure if this does occur. Correct the temperature and many of the corals can recover over time by recovering lost zooxanthellae or coralline algae. Feeding your bleached coral zooplankton can help keep them alive until their zooxanthellae is recovered.

Brown Jelly Infections

This necrosis occurs from coral warfare. Corals stinging the others for space and from rapid changes in the environment. These infected areas are a bacterial protozoa called Helicostoma sp. Feeding on decaying or dead tissue. Treatment freshwater dips and a quarantine tank. The coral's tissue will begin to recover.

Rapid Tissue Necrosis

This rarely occurs in the nano reef, but more often with acropora sp. Necrosis is more likely to occur in lps corals, starting from the base. The cause for this is still unknown but a variety of bacteria can be found after necrosis occurs. A bare skeleton is usually what's left behind. Quarantine is a good idea of the infected specimen in case of spreading or contagion.

Treatment

Chloroquine Phosphates: This is a new cure for Amyloodinium, Cryptocaryon, Uronema and Brooklynella. This treatment has proven more effective than copper and formalin and less toxic! It may be difficult to find but worth having in the fish medicine cabinet.

Copper: Copper is an effective treatment for Amyloodinium, Protozoa and Cryptocaryon irritans. Never treat with copper in the nano reef. Copper is toxic to invertebrates and difficult to remove even with large water changes. Use a quarantine/hospital tank to treat for illness.

Formalin: Formalin is used for ectoparasites and fish monogeneans. Affective with a fresh water dip. Formalin treats marine ich (Cryptocaryon irritans) and Velvet (Amyloodinium ocellatum).

Methylene Blue: This treatment is effective for fungal infections and as a fungicide for fish eggs. Also effective with a fresh water dip for fish and can increase oxygen in the water and reduce stress. Around two drops per gallon.

Hydrogen Peroxide: Hydrogen Peroxide has many uses in the nano tank. It can be a disinfecting agent on fish wounds and can be applied out of the water and directly to these wounds or in a quarantine/hospital tank. 0.10ml per 5 gallons for sensitive species or 0.25ml for more hardy marine species. It also acts as a fungicide or a protozoaside and in case of power outages, 1ml per 10 gallons every 6 hours will maintain oxygen levels. You can also add one drop in shipping bags, this will increase shipping time with increased oxygen levels. Hydrogen Peroxide also acts as an oxidizing agent and can help break down organic waste. Use caution, over dosing can kill beneficial bacteria and some corals and invertebrates may be sensitive to these slight over doses. Hydrogen Peroxide is a important part of the fish cabinet. A 3% solution can be found almost anywhere!

Chapter 4

Food and Live Food Culture

Feeding is an important part of fish health and well-being! Fish and invertebrates, if maintained properly with proper nutrition, will aid in color, vitality, growth and development, breeding and overall health and behavior. So understanding different species needs and diets can go along way with maintaining marine life. Proteins, carbohydrates, lipids, vitamins and minerals are all an important part and these can be supplemented with flakes, freeze-dried foods, frozen foods, and live foods. I will only be discussing live foods and their culture in this book.

Proteins and Carbohydrates

The diet of marine fish protein makes up 25% to 55% herbivores being at the lower end of the protein intake. Proteins are not something the fish can store in applicable amounts like fats. So regular protein intake is essential. Proteins can be found in plants and animals or in the transference from plant to animal and in saying that animal protein is more complete. Here is a depiction of this cycle.

Marine Proteins

Marine proteins are the healthiest forms of proteins. They're high in amino acids and lipids or fish oil, highly unsaturated fatty acids are rich in Omega 3 and Omega 6. Carbohydrates are nutrients that are made up of sugars and starches and fibers may be utilized by chemical conversions into sugar and absorbed as a high energy source. Carbohydrates are primarily plant based. Some fish like carnivores use less carbohydrates and herbivores use much more.

Lipids

Lipids are oils from animal, marine fish, and shrimp and other marine life produce highly unsaturated fatty acids or HUFAs. These types of oils or fats are a rich source of Omega 3 and Omega 6 and are critical for growth and development and breeding and the general health and well-being of your fishes or invertebrates. Lipids also aids in cell repair of damaged tissue.

Vitamins

Vitamins act as a catalyst for biochemical functions and also aids in growth and development and can be absorbed through food intake such as flora or fana and deficiencies can cause physical ailments such as deformity and can increase stress in the body of animals in question and can leave them open to disease.

Minerals

Minerals are mostly absorbed through water intake and can be utilized through regular water changes and mud filters are very helpful. Minerals aid with bone formation and hemoglobin production. Iodine deficiency is the most commonly seen. Goiter is a result of iodine deficiency.

Live Food Culture

Marine life is high in HUFAs, Omega 3 and Omega 6. By adding Macro algae and micro algae washed in fresh water and dried, provides a steady source for these nutrition's and adding fish or krill oil and vitamins will increase HUFA, Omega 3 and Omega 6 for mealworms, white worms, red earthworms, mosquito larva, confused beetles, fruit flies, feeder fish, feeder shrimp, copepods, amphipods, moina will all feed on these algae mixed in with their food.

Fruit Flies

Flightless fruit flies make a great supplemental food for your fish and invertebrates. Drosophila hydei is larger than Dosophila melanogaster. They're both easy to culture in plastic or glass jars with cheese cloth screen cover. knitting plastic mesh for them to crawl on in there container and for easy retrieval of the flies. They can be fed fruit, sugars, baby cereal and dried macro alga mix in with the other foods and a multivitamin.

Confused Beetles or Flour Beetles (Tribolium confusum)

Confused beetles are these annoying little beetles you find in your pancake mix or flour. They look similar to a mini mealworm. They have even been found in the pyramids. 4,000 year old beetles in the tombs of the pharaoh kings. They can be cultured in jars covered in cheese cloth. They can be fed flour, corn meal, baby cereal and crushed macro algae mixed with the other food dusted with multivitamins and a potato for water. You can sift with a screened strainer to feed to your fish the beetle larva are eaten most often and can help with these finicky feeders to start eating.

Mealworms

Mealworms are a good supplemental food. They are easily cultured in a plastic container. They will eat almost anything, cornmeal, baby cereal, oatmeal and dry macro algae mixed in with multivitamins and fruits or vegetables like potatoes for water. Most fish love them and can be fed at various sized beetle larva. They may help to get finicky feeders to eat.

Red Earth Worms (Lumbricus sp.)

The red earth worms are more tolerant of warm temperatures. Regular earth worms can be cultures the same way but will require a refrigerator or a cool basement. They can be cultured with potting soil, oatmeal and dried macro algae, maybe eaten mixed with other foods. Earth worms are a very fatty food source and are more of a supplement food. They are a good way to get finicky feeders to eat and they can be fed at all sizes. The red earth worm only grows about three inches.

White Worms, Grendal Worms, Micro Worms

These worms can all be cultured the same way but white worms are less tolerant of warm temperatures. These worms are easy to culture on potting soil without fertilizer or on peat moss in plastic storage boxes. A piece of glass or plexi-glass or a mirror should be placed on the surface of the soil with food underneath. The worms will stick to the glass and scraped off and are easily fed this way. They can be fed baby cereal or oatmeal with crushed macro algae mix with multivitamins. These worms are fatty and more of a supplement. A great way to get finicky feeders to eat and to stimulate breeding your marine fish.

Vinegar Worms

Vinegar worms are very small, possibly smaller than newly hatched brine shrimp and may serve as a prea brine shrimp food and are good supplemental food for fry, small fish and corals. They are easy to culture in a plastic or glass jar in Cider Vinegar. The worms ball up on the bottom and can be collected with a brine shrimp net or coffee filter and rinsed in fresh water.

Mosquito Larvae

Mosquito Larvae are a great supplement food for fish and invertebrates and can be cultured in a five gallon bucket that they lay their eggs raft in. They need grass clippings or hay, this will cause infusoria to grow. They will also eat bacteria and ditritas. They're a fatty food source and a great way to get finicky feeders to eat and stimulate fish breeding. This is free food source and you're getting rid of mosquitoes in your neighborhood.

Moina

Moina and are 50 to 70% rich with fatty acids. Moina are desert and plains plankton and live in vernal pools or salt flats and can survive in salt water for extended period. Moina reproduce two ways one is a- sexually and the other is when their vernal pools start to dry up the females produce males, and reproduce sexually. They lay ephippa or resting eggs and these eggs will survive. This dry period until the rains return and floods their little world again! They are tolerant of extremes and can be found across the southwestern US and Australia. There are smaller strains of Moina then are available and if someone finds a smaller cultures then they may prove beneficial to marine fish larvae or fry. They can be fed green algae water or a algae paste hi in HUFAS and omega-3 and omega-6. Moina reproduce prolifically and are easily sustainable.

Cyclops Freshwater Copepods

Freshwater copepods are a rich food source for marine fish and their fry and tend to reproduce more rapidly. They can be fed algae rich in HUFAs and possible cultured spirulina or possible marine algae that are rich in HUFAs. Some are desert dwelling that live in seasonal vernal pools and survive the dry season as ephippa or resting eggs. There are some very small freshwater copepod species and some may prove to be a good food source for marine fish, fry larva and may help advance pelagic larva rearing past metamorphosis stages. Marine copepods are one of the best food sources for your fry larvae and fish. They can be fed green algae water or paste. Copepods are a rich source for HUFAS, omega 3 and omega 6. Copepods don't reproduce as quickly as Moina or brine shrimp. You may need to have several cultures going at once and feed properly and proper water flow and regular water change. Your culture should be sustainable. Marine copepods can be cultured the same way but in sea water.

Amphipods or Scuds

Amphpods are a good source of nutrition for many fish like seahorses, pipefish and leaf scorpion fish. They're easily cultured in a sump or a tank of their own with macro algae and will eat algae paste or spirulina flakes. They reproduce fairly quickly and there are fresh water or marine species.

Brine Shrimp

Brine shrimp are a poor source of nutritional value and HUFAS. Except for newly hatched brine shrimp they will need to be gut loaded with green algae water or algae paste high in HUFAS, omega 3 and omega 6, but are one of the main food sources for fish fry, copepods and Moina are a better starter food source and brine shrimp as a supplement food.

Mysis Shrimp (Mysis sp.)

Freshwater mysis shrimp are a great stable food source for marine life. They can be cultured in a 10-gallon tank. They can be fed Moina or newly hatched brine shrimp gut loaded with green algae water or algae paste. These are high in HUFAs, omega 3 and omega 6. With regular water changes your culture will thrive.

Live Feeder Shrimp Culture

There are several different shrimp species that are fairly easy to culture. Some are freshwater some are salt or brackish water. Some of these are ghosts or grass shrimp Palaemonetes some species are freshwater and marine or brackish water. Neo and Bee shrimp are mostly freshwater but there are a few marine species but most of these three species have non pelagic larva. The easiest way to raise larvae shrimp is to separate the female with eggs and then remove the female after hatching Palaemonetes Species are more cannibalistic. The larvae of most will feed on algae or spirulina based diet and may also feed on crushed flakes foods and may also feed on newly hatched brine shrimp and Moina. This mostly applies to Palaemonetes sp, all food should be HUFAS loaded. Marine shrimp, Lysmata sp., Stenopus sp. and a few like Thor amoinensis and Lysmata wurdemanni have smaller larvae and are somewhat more contankterus to raise. All can be raised in a kriesal tank or circular container. The larvae can be fed green water or a algae paste and rotifers small then large strains and then brain shrimp and moina nauplii larva and copepod nauplii and will settle on the bottom in about two weeks to a month. All foods should be high in HUFAS. One advantage is the shrimp can be fed at various sizes and are easy to freeze for later use.

Live Feeder Fish

There are many species that can be raised as a food source, mollies, guppies and mosquito fish like Gambusia rhizophorae. The mangrove mosquito fish is native to South Florida. These fish can be fed at various sizes or frozen and chopped into bite size pieces and fed at a later date. All should be gut loaded with HUFAS rich foods.

Rotifers

There are two types of rotifers that are commonly cultured. The large strain (Brachionus plicatilis) and the small strain (Brachionus plicatilis). Rotifers can be cultured with a green algae paste or green algae water, be careful of algae paste with yeast, these can cause unstable cultures that will produce cilates that will out compete rotifers and cause your cultures to crash. That is why it is better to run several cultures at once. After green algae water is added in 5 to 7 days, the rotifer cultures will turn brown and the rotifers are ready for harvesting. More green algae water should be added and new culture started bi-weekly because of dead rotifers, this will also cause unstable cultures. There should be a 50% ratio of rotifers with eggs. This is a good indication of a healthy culture. Rotifers are an important first food because most marine fish larvae are too small to eat copepods, nepali moina, nepali brine shrimp but they should be fed as soon as possible. They are more nutritious than rotifers and they should be oxygenated without a air stone.

Cilates

Cilates are what cause red tides but some are safe for food cultures as a fry larvae fish food most cilates are a little smaller than rotifers and this makes them a likely food source. The culture's are easily started, all you need is a rotifer culture and some yeast and the cilates will take over rapidly and should be harvested in 5 to 7 days. Use caution with fri larvae cilates can deplete oxygen Levels in their tank small portions are ok with rotifers.

Green Water Algae Culture

Micro Algae are the main source of HUFAs for your marine life. Often they are fed to your zooplankton like copepods, brine shrimp, moina and are then fed to your fish and so on. Some of the most common are Nannochloropsis sp and Isochrysis sp. The easiest way to culture them is in two or three liter bottles washed out with hydrogen peroxide and an airline running into the lid running at a slower pace for oxygen exchange. The cultures can be fed marine fertilizers with minor trace elements and phosphorous added at a ratio of 10:1 bright lighting with full spectrum bulbs very close.to the bottle is important for rapid cultures.

Macro Algae Culture

Macro algae is a good food source for marine life, they are also full of Omega 3 and Omega 6 and other nutrients. They grow rapidly and are easy to culture in a sump under a bright light or in the main reef tank. For feeding, they should be frozen first, this helps break them down or drying them out is another option. They can be mixed in with other foods like frozen blocks of Gracilaria sp, Enteromorpha sp are good starter Macro cultures.

Coralline Algae Family Corallinaceae

There are many different species of encrusting Coralline algae or zooxanthella and corals also have a preference of which species they absorb and grow in their tissue through photosynthesis. Coroline algae provides most of their coral host food energy with sugar starch enzymes. They typically come in pink, red or purple but are also seen in blue, white, grey, green and yellow. Coralline algae also share a symbiotic relationship with other marine animals like tridacna clams. There are primary Coralline deposit is calcite and all species are of a marine origin. High temperatures can cause bleaching and cause the host coral to expel their Corolline algae and turn white or clear color. Some corals can survive by absorbing strong or more heat tolerant strains of coralline algae of that corals preference of zooxanthella or coralline algae. This can help corals to recover in the wild and possibley grow stronger more adaptive coral reefs.

Chapter 5

Bonsai Trees for the Mini Reef

Mangrove Trees

Mangrove trees are some of the most unusual and beautiful trees. They grow with a tap root submerged in the sea and with upper air roots to prevent them from drowning. They excrete salt out of a few leaves that turn yellow and this helps them deal with excess salt. They grow propagals that eventually fall in the sea and drift off to start a new tree. These propagals range from similar to a lima bean to long thin rod. These are what we grow in our nanos. They do well under bright lighting and with a coral reef below, they can be pruned and wired. There is flexwire that has plastic coating and this should stay on the tree for 3 to 6 months just like any bonsai tree for the desired look and to reduce shadowing the reef below. They look great in tidal tanks and can grow in your homemade live rock with piping or holes for them to grow in. They should be provided with nutrition rich mud and overall they are easy to care for and complete the bonsai nano reef.

1. The Red Mangrove Tree (Rhizophora mangle)
   These trees are one of the most popular of the mangroves kept in reef tanks. They have long and thin propagules. These are starter tree pods. They grow under bright lighting light green leaves with blunt points and a waxy look. Their bark has a greyish color and is dark red underneath. Their pneumatophore air roots grow long and thin.

2. The Black Mangrove Tree (Avicennia germinans)
   These mangrove trees have elliptical long leaves that are covered with hairs on the underside. There pneumatophore air roots are long and thin. They grow propagules that look similar to lima beans and are about 1 inch and are a little more difficult to get started growing but once you do, they grow well.

3. The White Mangrove Tree (Laguncularia racemosa)
   These pretty mangrove trees grow peg air roots that are short and stocky, more than any other species. They grow broad leaves and are oval at both ends. They produce lima bean looking propaguls that are about 0.2 inch and can be somewhat difficult to grow, but once growing they do well.

4. The Buttonwood Tree (Conocarpus erectus)
   These are nice looking trees not technically a mangrove but growing in a similar way with roots wet maybe a little shallow water. They have pointed leaves that have salt glands that excrete excess salt. Their bark has somewhat rough texture and they flower with button seed cases that germinate on the mother tree. These trees grow at a slow pace but are definitely worth your time and fairly easy to grow. Sea Buck thorn Sea buckthorn (Hippophae sp.).

5. Eleannacae (Oleaster Family)
   Te sea buckthorn is named for its ability to withstand seashore conditions, where it's abundant, bright orange berries and willowy silver leaves add color to a bleak landscape. The fruit is acidic It is not devoured by birds. It rarely grows large and will grow well as a bonsai tree, both male and female trees are needed to produce fruit. Hardy in zone 3 to 8. They will grow in most any soil and are salt tolerant Partial shade to full sun. They are difficult to transplant young plants and cuttings or seeds are easier to transplant. No serious pest or diseases.

6. The Lili-Pili Tree (Syzygium smithii)
   These evergreens grow 25 feet in the wild. They have salt tolerant leaves that are a reddish chocolate brown in new growth. They turn dark green. They grow not overly flavorful red edible berries. They are used to make jelly and drinks in their native land of Australia and New Zealand. They grow in sub-tropical rainforest and dry forest near streams. They are hardy trees. They have clusters of small white flowers. They do well under moderate to bright lighting and warm temperatures.

7. Rainbow Eucalyptus Tree (Eucalyptus deglupta)
   The rainbow tree grows tall and upright in the wild up to 6 feet wide and 200 or more feet tall. They grow in humid rainforests. These hard wood trees are native to southeast Asia and Australia and are not cold tolerant. They are used for making paper. The rainbow tree grows well with moist to wet rich soil and mild fertilizer. They prefer bright lighting and have lance shaped leaves and are evergreens. The leaves are also aromatic and the rainbow tree grows tiny white flowers. The bark peels and it is smooth underneath. The rainbow tree has colorful maroon red, green, blue, purple, orange and grey. The bark is more colorful under fabrable condions. They have no pest problems and can be propagated from seeds or root side shoots. They make beautiful bonsai trees and formal upright is the most common but other bonsai styles can be grown. Salt splash is less tolerant.

The Desert Bonsai Nano Reef

There are many deserts by the sea and many deserts are filled with beautiful and unusual plants and even though they can't grow in water, they can grow on the rock work in and around the nano reef. The setting can be anything from the Baja peninsula or the Mediterranean Coast or desert islands. Some of the most beautiful reefs are from desert regions with minimum run off from rivers or rain. All desert reefs require bright lighting and minimum watering and organic fertilizer on occasion. This can be a rare and beautiful display and many desert plants are salt spray tolerant.

Desert Bonsai Trees

The beautiful colorful purples leucophyllum can make a wonderful bonsai tree and bloom almost year round. They require bright to moderately bright lighting, a little fresh water once or twice a week, a weak organic fertilizer once every month. Leucophyllum are from the north american south west and mexico desert and may benefit from a winter cooling to induce flower blooms. This can be done if they are planted in small pots in the rock work and removed for a cool spell.

Acacia

Acacia's make nice bonsai trees. Many species have small leaves and may have puff ball yellow flowers. The sweet Acacia (Vachellia farnesiana) is one of my favorites. They require bright lighting and should be planted in small pots in the rock work and removed for short cooling periods if you want to increase blooms the following year.

Blue Palo Verde (Parkinsonian florida)

These beautiful trees have yellow flowers and are bright almost lime green color including their trunks. They do best in bright lighting and a little fresh water once or twice a week, a weak organic fertilizer once a month and may benefit from a cooling period, this will increase blooms.

Ground Cover

Desert Verbena can make good ground cover with their small stature and green foliage and pinky purple and white flowers. They require bright to moderately bright lighting, a little fresh water once or twice a week and weak organic fertilizer once a month. They may benefit from a cooling period to increase flower blooms. They can be propagated from cuttings or seeds. They should be trimmed to desired shape.

Succulents-Cacti Sedumpachyphllum

These red tipped, green succulents stand semi upright. They grow more red under bright lighting and are known as the booze nose. They grow small yellow flowers.

Chinese Lantern Plant (Ceropegia sp.)

These are an attractive Linearis triling succulent. They have small flowers. They prefer bright lighting and water twice a week and less in winter. They have pretty variegated leaves and they can be lightly fertilized once or twice a month in Summer, none in Winter. A slight cool down will help with flowering the next Spring and should be in a pot for easy removal. For this cool down of 6 so at leased. Can be propagated from cutting in sotso mix sand and soil.

Gherkin Cactus (Echinopsis chamaecereus)

These pretty cacti from West Argentina is a cascading plant with beautiful pink or red flowers. They do well in moderate bright light, maybe a little farther away from the light. They prefer slightly cooler temperatures so a house is usually a good temperature. The Summers water well once a week and les the plant dry between watering and once every three weeks in the Winter or reduce temperature. This will increase flowering the next Spring. Best kept in pots. Propagated easily from cutting or seeds they may take 20 days to germinate after a resting or storage period of the seeds a week. Fertilize once a month in the Summer, Sotso mix, soil and sand.

Aloe Gonialoe variegata

These aloes can grow around 6 inches but propagate cuttings can be changed out if they grow too large for your nano. They do well under moderate bright light. They should be watered up to twice a week. They grow well in 75% soil and 25% sand. Water less in a cooling or mild Wintering. They often flower during this time. They can also be grown from seed.

Chameleons

If you use a fogger or mist on a daily basis. The out crop rocks with plants and small trees, keeping dwarf chameleons is possible. There are two types I will mention here, the Dwarf Jackson's Chameleon (Chamaeleo jacksonii merumontanus), which grow up to three inches head to vent and the Kenya pygmy chameleon (Rieppeleon Kerstenii), they grow to about two inches. Chameleons can be trained to eat out of your fingers or a small bowl. Chameleons usually want drop from their tree or ground or rock so an open top nano tank is ok. The trees can even hang over the side of the fish tank and if the chameleon falls in the water, they can swim a little back to the rocks. You can have outer plexi-glass barrier and have rock work and plants all around the nano reef tank. You can even have a separate fresh waterfall wrapping around the nano tank with a small pump and plant a tree growing down the side. Use caution with more than one chameleon, this can stress them very much.

Macro Algae

Macro Algae are a diverse group of lower order of plants. They come in many forms and are colorful. A nano tank full of these beautiful algae and corals is something to see. Most are easy to grow and some seem to benefit from Calcium, Iron and trace elements. Many species of Macro Algae grow in shallow seas. They require a moderate to bright lighting with a Kelvin temperature of around 5000K to 10,000K. Macro Algae are a great food source for marine life. They help remove waste or proteins, ammonia nitrates and nitrates. They produce oxygen for the nano reef tank. They are also great in sumps over mineral mud as filtration. Macro algae has been known to drop the Ph overnight if the lights are off, but it's my opinion that this has little effect on the reef and if you look at the wild corals and large macro algae fields grow just fine together and it's natural.

Mermaid Fan (Udotea sp.)

These algae are attractive green fun shaped! They seem to prefer moderate bright lighting and it helps them grow well with Calcium, Iron and trace elements. They grow well on rocks or gravelly sand with moderate to rapid water flow. Nitrates and phosphates can cause algae to grow on the leaves. The mermaid fan does well with lps and sps corals with higher Calcium needs and lighting.

Turtle Grass Maidens Hair (Chlorodesmis sp.)

These macro algae are filamentous grass like and green in color. They contain a toxic deterent that help reduce herbivore marine life from eating them. Turtle grass matts makes great place for spawning and for fry to grow and hide in. They do best under moderate to bright lighting and moderate to rapid water flow. They seem to benefit from Iron and trace elements. They are sensitive to high nitrates and copper.

Merman's Shaving Brush (Penicillus sp.)

These attractive algae have brisal leaves and grow well on live rocks or gravel sand. They grow best under moderately bright light and moderate to rapid water flow. They're a little difficult to get started but once established, they do well with good Calcium levels, Iron and trace elements. This makes them a good companion with lps and sps corals.

Tufted Joint Algae (Cymopolia barbara)

These algae are found throughout the Gulf of Mexico and beyond. There are hardy algae and require moderate care and grow well in moderate to bright light and medium water flow. High nitrates ad phosphates can cause algae to grow on them. They benefit from Magnesium, Iron and trace elements and are a good food source for marine life. They also do well with lps and sps corals in a slack water flow area of the nano tank.

Halimeda sp.

These algae are reef builders and are calcareous. They are sometimes called the cactus of the sea. They're light green and have rough exteriors. They require bright lighting and modern to rapid water flow. High nitrates and phosphates can cause algae to grow on them! They require Calcium, Iron and trace elements and are a good choice for lps and sps corals.

Gracilaria sp.

These macro algae are pretty reds and pinks and fast growing and help reduce nitrates and phosphates and are a great food source for marine life. They seem to benefit from Iron, Magnesium and trace elements and give off a pleasant sea smell!

Grape Kelp (Botryocladia sp.)

This grape leafed kelp is a pretty red and they are fast growing but can be trimmed down and they're a good food source for herbivore marine life. They are from the indo-pacific. They require moderate to bright lighting and moderate to rapid water flow. The grape kelp seems to benefit from Calcium, Iron and trace elements.

Kelp (Haliptilon sp.)

The smooth leaf kelp is a deeper water algae and grow up to 10 inch strands that are free swaying in moderate to rapid water current. They need medium to bright light and are fairly easy to grow and have beautiful red color and are a great marine life food source and help reduce nitrates and phosphates in the nano tank! They also give off a pleasant sea smell!

Rhodophyta sp. Kelp

This beautiful kelp is purple in color and grow strand like up to 10 inches or more. They are fern like in appearance. They do best under moderate to bright lighting and moderate to rapid water flow. They are from the Indo-Pacific. These macro algae seem to benefit from Calcium, Iron and trace elements.

Caulerpa Algae

These fast growing macro algae are attractive and some look like waving seagrass like C. prolifera or green grapes like C. mexicana Caulerpa grow by vining across the bottom and over rocks with small roots attaching at the base of their nodes. These are easy macro algae to grow. They can be cut back easily and help remove proteins from the water like nitrates. They do best in moderate to bright lighting and moderate to rapid water flow. They are eaten by some herbivore fish and invertebrates. They also grow well in mineral muds and sumps for filtration.

Chapter 6   Fishes

Fishes are the backbone to any tank and this in the literal sense because they're usually the only animal in the tank with a back bone. Fish come in a ray of colors, shapes and sizes. They have different personalities, even fish of the same species! Their beauty captivates us. Some resemble lizards and even leaves like the ghost pipe fish. Their wonder fascinates us. Marine fish are now starting to be breed and raised in captivity and are proving to be more adaptive then their wild counter parts. The love for the hobby must be sustainable in order for it to keep going.

Fry Care and Breeding

Demersal spawners are typically nest builders that dig pits in the sand or clean a rock or cave to lay eggs in. Most Demersal Spawners are breed in nano tanks. Many lay a group of eggs and some lay single eggs one at a time and some lay gelatinous blobs or ribbon egg strands and others are mouth breeders and many of the nest builders lay larger eggs. Some have no pelagic stage and hatch out as tiny versions of their parents. Most have pelagic stage called larvae fry. This stage lasts about 25 to 40 days. These pelagic larvae stay in the water column throughout this stage before metamorphosis and settling on the reef.

Broad Cast Spawners

Most Broad Cast Spawners breed in huge tanks! They rise up in the water column and expel large amounts of sperm and tiny eggs with oil globules that keep them buoyant, sometimes ranging in the millions. Most hatch out and float and drift and hatch out as tiny pro-larvae with large yolk sacs. That helps keep them buoyant. Their larval stage is extended from 35 to 80 days and are much harder to raise because of their need for very small foods.

Fry and Shrimp Larvae Care

Most marine pelagic fish and shrimp larvae are raised in kriesel or circular containers that range from 10 to 20 gallons and are usually removed with the rock they are laid on the night of hatching. The fry eye up in the eggs and you know it's time to transfer them. The reason you wait until the last is the male is usually their care taker and blows water at them and fans them and removes fused eggs and this increases hatch rates and fry size. Another way to remove fry is a fish trap. These are at the surface with a light that draws the fry in a trap and circulation then around and round until you put them in their larvae tank. Put them in slowly and with the water from the parent's tank. Make sure water parameters are the same as the parent's tank and add fry slowly. The fry need to be kept in close contact with their food if you want them to live past the pelagic stage and metamorphic. The water in their fry tank should have a slow to medium flow, this helps the fry find their food. Some losses are expected but over time and several egg clutches, your fry survival rate will increase and your skills will be honed over several broods!

Small Fry Feeding

Small fry eats small strain rotifers, strombidium, cilates and 5 to 10 days later large strain rotifers, and 13 to 20 days later or as soon as possible, moinas nauplii, brine shrimp nauplii. They are much higher in HUFAs, Omega 3 and Omega 6 which are essential for fry survival, growth and development.

Large Fry Feeding

Large fry will eat large strain rotifers as a starter food but copepods nauplii, moina nauplii and brine shrimp nauplii are much richer in HUFAs, Omega 3 and Omega 6 which will aid in fry survival, growth and development and should be changed over as soon as possible. This is usually 7 to 15 days.

Grow Out Tanks

Grow out tanks are usually 50 or more gallons and these can be fish tanks or large heavy duty plastic containers. The fry losses will reduce at this stage. Between 35 to 80 days after metamorphosis and then culling of deformed or inferior, fry must take place. The fry can be weaned onto flake and small frozen foods at this time.

Seahorses (Hippocampinae sp.)

Seahorses really are truly amazing creatures. They have the head of a horse, a prehensile tail, color changing ability, independent eye movement, their armor plated and the males are the ones that give live birth from their pouch. There are at least 60 species of Hippocampinae sp, this subfamily is part of Syngnathidae sp. There are over 250 species in this family, this includes pipefish, trumpet fish, sea dragons and seahorses. The largest is the giant pacific seahorse (Hippocampus ingens), they grow up to 14 inches and one of the smallest. The pygmy seahorse (Hippocampus satomiae). They top out at about a quarter of an inch. Medium to small seahorses do best in a nano that's tall! This keeps them in close proximity to their food! Tall nanos are recommended at least 3 times the seahorse's height for breeding! Seahorses rise up into the water column. This helps with successful copulation.

Most seahorses are captive bred and are more adaptive to feed on frozen foods like mysis shrimp. Seahorses have small stomachs and need to be fed two or three times a day. Dwarf seahorses are less likely to eat frozen foods and prefer living moving food. The pipe and bowl feeding method as mentioned earlier in the book is recommended and they will associate the bowl with food and make feeding easier. Most seahorses do best in moderate water flow, this also helps them find their food and most are not strong swimmers. They do well with dead sea fans and branches and macro algae. These provide resting places for your seahorses to perch. Seahorses do fine with soft an lps corals long as they don't have strong stinging nematocyst. Live Sea Fans are beautiful but use many other places for the Seahorses to rest. Over perched sea fans can cause tissue die off! Companions for seahorses have to be slow moving fish with smaller mouths like Leaf scorpionfish (Taenianotus triacanthus) or pipefish and small starfish like the spotted linka starfish, Red Fromia Starfish with medium size seahorses or asterina starfish and micro brittle starfish with small seahorses like the dwarf seahorse. Snails and small tradacnid clams or hermit crabs, these all do well with little trouble.

Dwarf Seahorses (Hippocampus zosterae)

Dwarf seahorses are one of my favorite ponies. They grow up to about 1 inch or so. A pair can be kept in as small 2 gallon nano tank with good filtration. They can be kept around 68 to 78 degrees. They prefer live food but may be weened onto frozen food. Newly hatched brine shrimp are the stable but moina and copepods are eaten as well. They can be fed 2 to 3 times a day, but don't over feed, this can raise nitrates and phosphates in your nano! Dwarf seahorses usually breed on their own and can be kept with their parents. The baby seahorses will eat newly hatched brine shrimp and can e kept with their parents. Dwarf seahorses are sensitive to hydroid infestations, hydroids are closely related to jellyfish, larger seahorses seem to handle them better. Their stinging nematocyst are what effects the dwarf seahorses and can end in high mortality rates with baby seahorses. Hydroids are usually introduced with live rock. They have free swimming jellyfish stages that settles on the rocks. These can look like small anomones, some grow solitarily and others are colonial and resemble a spider web. So use caution when introducing new rocks, corals and macro algae.

The Pug Nosed Seahorse (Hippocampus breviceps)

These ponies grow about 3 inches and they are a hardy species. They require a cool water nano around 65 to 70 degrees so a chiller may be needed. These prolific ponies have about 30 or so fry. They have large babies and have no pelagic stage and feed on brine shrimp nauplii, copepods, moina. The adults will eat frozen mysis shrimp. The pug nosed seahorses are a great starter species into a temperate reef and up to 5 can be kept in a 15 gallon nano tank.

The Tubers Seahorse (Hippocampus tuberculatus)

These ponies grow to about 3 or 4 inches and are hardy cool water species! They do best around 65 to 74 degrees. These little ponies have long cirri and long tubers like eye lashes! They eat frozen mysis shrimp, and they have hardy fry that are non-pelagic that will also eat smaller frozen foods like small mysis shrimp, brine shrimp, moina, and copepods. The tubers seahorses will do well as long as they're fed often and up to 5 can be kept in a 15 or 20-gallon temperate reef tank.

The Cape Seahorse (Hippocampus capensis)

These ponies are from South Africa and have one of the smallest ranges in the wild are a hardy species and breed well and have large non-pelagic fry that feed well on brine shrimp nauplii, copepods, and moina. The adults will eat frozen mysis shrimp. They don't require a heater and 65 to 70 degrees is ideal. They grow to about 3 or 4 inches and up to 5 can be kept in a 15 to 20-gallon reef!

The Hawaiian Seahorse (Hippocampus fisheri)

These little guys grow to about 2 or 3 inches and are oceanic explorers. They do fine around 70 to 75 degrees. They will eat small mysis shrimp, brine shrimp, copepods and moina. They're a little harder to ween onto frozen food. They give birth to large broods as many as 1.500 fry that are pelagic and tiny and are difficult to raise. The fry will feed on large strain rotifer =, brine shrimp nauplii, copepod nauplii and moina nauplii. The Hawaiian seahorses are a very pretty pony, they can range in color from pinkish, reds, golden orange and yellows. These pelagic seahorses need a larger nano because they're more active. A 15 to 20-gallon open reef will do nicely for up to 5 ponies.

(Hippocampus kuda)

These Hardy mid size horses grow to around 4 or 6 inches and do fine at 68 to 78 degrees. The adults will eat frozen mysis shrimp and the fri will eat brine shrimp nauplii, copepod nauplii and moina nauplii. The males give birth to around 200 fri and the baby sea horses have about a two week pelagic stage. These horses are a good specie's to begin advancing your fri rearing skills. There a little more difficult then the lined sea horse (Hippocampus erectus). These pretty seahorses are usually yellow or orange, red, black and brown are also seen. Three or four kuda sea horses can be kept in a 15 or 20 gallon nano tank.

The Lined Seahorse (Hippocampus Erectus)

These stout and hardy medium size horses do very well home on the range. These are very good starter species and come in many different color varieties; orange, red, purple, greenish, maroon, grey, black, yellow, gold, lavender, lilac and peach! These seahorses are fine around 56 to 78 degrees. The adults can be fed frozen mysis shrimp. The fry will eat brine shrimp nauplii, copepods, and moina. The lined seahorses are hardy at reproducing. They have 250 to 1500 fry in a single brood and hardy babies, the main problem is keeping all these mouths fed. Fed properly a 60% to 80% or more survival rate is possible. The babies sexually mature 4 to 5 inches. They do well on the reef and you can keep 3 or 4 in a 15 gallon nano reef tank.

Hippocampus jayakari

These seahorses are from the Indian Ocean, the Red Sea and the Arabian Sea. They are usually found at a depth of around 9 feet but can be found up to 60 feet deep. They are usually found in seagrass beds. They grow up to 5 ¾ inches. They can be fed mysis shrimp. Their temperature range should be 68 to 78 degrees. Three or four in a tall 15 or 20-gallon nano reef tank will do well.

The Brazilian Seahorse (Hippocampus Reidi)

These very colorful seahorses grow 6 to 8 inches and are more delicate than other species and require good water quality and filtration. They do well with a temperature of 68 to 78 degrees. The adults can be fed mysis shrimp. They have large broods 300 to 2000 with tiny fry that are more difficult to raise. The fry can be fed large strain rotifers, brine shrimp nauplii, copepod nauplii and moina nauplii. Their fry have a lengthy pelagic stage up to 2 or 3 weeks. The Brazilian seahorse are often found on wild coral reefs and do well in a nano. A pair in a 15 or 20-gallon tank will look great and corals like gorgonian to the back to give them room for breeding and successful copulation.

The Emperor Seahorse (Hippocampus proceros)

The Emperor seahorses have five pointed cornet or crowns. They are variable in color but are often seen a yellowish color. They grow to about 4 ½ inches. There are endemic to tropical Australia around the coast of Queensland. They are endemic to tropical seagrass beds. They can be fed frozen mysis shrimp and are a hardy species. A tall 15 or 20-gallon reef tank can house up to four emperior seahorses.

The Thorny Seahorse (Hippocampus histrix)

The Thorny Seahorse is one of the larger species. They can grow up to 7.9 inches but are more typically around 6 inches. There wild counter part has one of the largest distribution. They are often found around 30 to 80 feet deep in the west Indi-Pacific Ocean. They have long snouts and are variable in color, but yellow, pink or green are the most commonly seen. A pair in a 15 to 20-gallon tall nano reef tank will do well. The taller corals like gorgonian should be grown toward the back of the nano. This leaves room for breeding and successful copulation. Their temperature range should be around 68 to 78 degrees.

The Tigertail Seahorse (Hippocampus comes)

This is a primarily nocturnal species. They are from the Indi-Pacific from Vietnam to Malaysia. They're a tropical seahorse and their temperature range should be 68 to 78 degrees. There often found on soft coral reefs. They can grow up to 7 ½ inches. The males are often black or a dark color and females are often yellowish in color. A pair in a tall 15 to 20-gallon nano reef will do well. The taller corals to the back. This will give them room to breed and for successful copulation. They can be fed mysis shrimp. The fry are on the larger side but can be difficult to raise. They can be fed copepod nauplii, moina nauplii and brine shrimp nauplii.

Hippocampus barbouri

These seahorses come from Southeast Asia, Indian and Pacific Oceans along the coast. They're found in shallow seagrass beds and mangrove swamps at a maximum depth of 3 feet. They grow up to 6 inches but the females are usually smaller. Their colors range from white, yellow, green, red, grey and brown. They may have reddish or brownish spots and some have lines on their body. They're a tropical species and their temperature range should be 68 to 78 degrees. Four can be kept in a tall 15 to 20-gllon nano reef tank. They will eat mysis shrimp and the male gives birth to non-pelagic fry any were from 10 to 250. They should be raised in a tank of their own. They will eat copepods, moina, brina shrimp nauplii.

Hippocampus Whitei

The white seahorse is from Australia. Their range is new south wales. Their color is often off white or cream color or yellow. They grow up to 8 inches. They prefer a temperature between 68 to 74 degrees. They can be fed mysis shrimp. Their fry are large and have non-pelagic stage. They have brood up to 200 fry. The fry can be fed copepods, moina and brine shrimp nauplii. Two or three in a tall 15 or 20-gallon ano reef will do well.

European Long Snouted Seahorse (Hippocampus guttulatus)

These seahorses are from the Northeast Atlantic and the Mediterranean Sea throughout the eastern basin usually in shallow waters in seagrass beds. They can grow up to 6 ½ inches. They are variable in color but are often yellow, red, brown or black and cirri. They prefer a temperature around 60 to 75 degrees but a drop in temperature ay help stimulate breeding. Their broods are between 150 to 900 fry. They have large fry with a short pelagic stage. They can be raised in a tank of their own and can be fed copepods, moina, and brine shrimp nauplii. The adults can be fed frozen mysis shrimp. Three or four in a tall 15 to 20-gallon nano reef tank will do well.

Hippocampus zebra

Endemic to Australia Queensland West-central pacific. Non-migratory likely large fry. Usually 20m in depth, found off shore near reefs. Size 3 1/2 to 4 inches. Males are larger. Yellowish-white and brown or blackish bands or stripes cover the head and body.

Pipefish (Syngnathidae)

Pipefish are a very interesting companions for seahorses and are often moving in and out of nooks and crannies. Many are very colorful and peaceful natured. They seem to prefer each other's company and get along well with other peaceful species that don't out complete them for food. They eat small mysis shrimp and different kinds of zooplankton. The females have rounder bellies and some species, the male have a pouch that the female deposits the eggs into. Some species the males have flat stomachs and the female deposits a strip of eggs on and they adhere to the male's belly. Pipefish often breed on their own, but the fry are very tiny and hard to raise. They will eat small zooplankton and can be raised in a Kriesel tank with small and large strain rotifers, cilates, brine shrimp nauplii, copepod nauplii, and moina. There are mainly two types of pipefish, belly sliders and the swimmers. Some of these consist of what are called flagtails. The belly sliders have a primitive prehensile tail and rap them around objects, usually close to the bottom. Most are fine with corals as long as they don't have strong stinging nematocysts and get along with most small invertebrates and all do well in a nano reef tank.

The Blue Stripe Dwarf Pipefish (Doryhamphus excisus)

The blue striped are small flagtail pipefish only 3 inches. They have a blue stripe and are a yellowish orange. This species makes a good companion with dwarf seahorses and will eat the same foods. They prefer 70 to 78 degree temperature. One male and three females do well. The female will lay her eggs on the male's stomach. They do well on the reef.

The Yellow Multi Banded Pipefish (Doryhamphus pessuliferus)

These colorful candy looking flagtails grow up to 6 ¼ inch, are black, red, white and yellow in color and are strong swimmers. They do well with medium seahorses and eat mysis shrimp. They prefer a temperature of 70 to 78 degrees. These pipefish can be kept in sexual pair or trio and the female lays eggs on the male's stomach. They do well in a larger nano reef.

Janss Pipefish (Doryrhamphus janssi)

These pipefish are blue and orange and grow to 5 ½ inches and are strong swimming flagtails. They prefer a temperature of 70 to 78 degrees and will eat mysis shrimp. They do well with medium seahorses. A sexual pair can be kept together or a trio. This species breeds regularly and the male carries the eggs on his stomach and should be kept in a large nano reef.

Dragonface Pipefish (Corythoichthys sp.)

These pipefish are variable in color and can be pink, white, yellow or black. They have unusual color patterns. They are belly sliders and slide swim around and through the reef. They will feed on most live shrimps and amphipods offered and can be adapted over to frozen foods. They reproduce with females attaching their eggs on the male flat belly. They will breed on a regular basis in the nano reef but fry will need to be moved to a kreisel tank to be raised but fry is difficult to rear out of larval stage. The Dragonface Pipefish grow to about 3 to 7 inches. Some of the most commonly seen are C. haematopterus and C. intestinalis.

Gobies

Gobies are ideal nano reef tank fish. Most are calm and good natured. Many are small and are happy even in a small nano. There are over 2,000 species of gobies and many from tropical seas so there is a great diversity to choose from. Some species have shrimp companions and others hop swim throughout the coral reefs.

Stonogobiops Shrimp Gobi (S. yasha) (S. nematodes)

Stonogobiops are pretty little gobies. Yasha is white with broken orange stripes and a large dorsal fin and yellowish dorsal, and caudal fins. The barber pole goby has a large dorsal fin and is an off white with a yellow head and slanted black brownish bars. These gobies have a close commensal relationship with pisal shrimp. The shrimp digs a burrow and the goby moves in with him. The pistol shrimp has poor eyesight and usually only comes out with his companion the goby. The gobies good eye sight the shrimp keeps one antenna on his goby friend and if danger approaches they dart back in their burrow and sometimes there can be a pair of gobies and three or more shrimp in one hole.

The Yellow Watchman Gobies (Crytocentrus cinctus)

These mellow yellow fellows are also a pistol shrimp goby! They're very hardy gobies! They grow to 3 or 4 inches and are captive bred! They will eat most types of fish foods and prefer temperatures 70 to 78 degrees. They do well in a 10-gallon nano reef for two! Other Crytocentrus sp can be kept the same way.

Coral Clown Gobies (Gobiodon sp.)

Clown gobies are some of the more entertaining. They dart about here and there in and out of the corals always after the best perch! They form social hierarches this way. They are bred often but have small fry and are hard to raise. The fry requires very small zooplankton and have a lengthy pelagic larvae stage. They start to color up about

33 to 40 days after metamorphosis. The adults will eat most foods offered. These gobies produce a toxic slime and are colorful. Three or four in a 10-gallon nano reef do well at a temperature of 70 to 78 degrees.

Blue Neon Gobies (Elacatinus oceanops)

These little gobies grow up to 2 inches. They're a cleaner goby and groom fish that could eat them. They can be kept 68 to 78 degrees. They will eat most foods offered and breed often on their own. They're a great starter fish for first time breeders and raising marine fish fri! These gobies lay between 50 to 250 eggs demersal usually on a rock surface. The fri require very small zooplankton and need to be raised in a kreisel tank. Their larval stage lasts about 26 to 45 days and they start to color up. The blue neon gobies do well on the nano reef 2 or 3 in a 5-gallon tank will do well. Their care applies to other species in their genus!

The Green Banded Goby (Tigrigobius multifasciatus)

These beauties are from the Caribbean and top out at about 2 inches. These gobies are often found in groups in tidel zones often with sea urchins and use them for protection. They fare at temperatures of 70 to 78 degrees. They will eat most foods offered. These gobies are commonly bred in captivity. These demersal spawners usually lay their eggs on rocks. They lay up to 250 eggs. The tiny fri can be raised in a kreisel. The fri can be fed very small zooplankton. They metamorphosis in 29 to 35 days and begin to color up. These gobies do well in a group and 4 or 5 in a 10-gallon nano reef.

The Flaming Prawn Goby (Discordipinna griessingeri)

The flaming prawn goby is a great candidate for the nano. These fish top out at an inch or less. They prefer live copepods and small amphipods. You can wean them onto frozen mysis shrimp, moina, copepods and brine shrimp. These gobies are shy at first and a small nano will keep them in view. Two or three in a 5-gallon nano reef should do well. Their temperature should be at 70 to 78 degrees. The flaming prawn gobies really are beautiful and are said to be a pistal shrimp companion. They're a great companion with dwarf seahorses as well!

Trimma sp. Gobies

Tremmia gobies make great nano tank fishes, they're tiny! They have calm personalities and like to sit and perch and wait for zooplankton to pass by. They will eat brine shrimp, copepods and moina and some flake foods. Trimmia tevegae is one of my favorites. The Japanese imports of this species are the most colorful. They do well at a temperature of 70 to 78 degrees. A pair can be kept in a 2-gallon nano reef.

The Green Pygmy (Eviota guttata) and others also make good nano fish.

Damsel fish (Pomacentridae)

Damselfish and cromis are in the family of (Pomacentridae). The clownfish are apart of this group in the subfamily (Amphiprionidae). This group perhaps are the most commonly kept group of marine fish. The clownfish have been bred longer than any other. There are several species that do well in a nano reef tank. They will eat most food offered and so it's easy to see why their a popular marine fish. Which ever you choose, you can't go wrong. Although many cromis grow a little large for all but the largest nano tank. Damsel fish are easy to breed but there fri are tiny larvae and difficult to raise out of the pelagic stage and through metamorphosis. The fri require very small zooplankton. It takes 3 or 4 days for Damsel fish eggs to hatch and around 30 days to metamorphosis. Clown fish eggs broods vary! Smaller specie's lay around 200 eggs and large species, up to 1,500 eggs. The pelagic fri larvae need to be fed very small zooplankton. The fri take between 25 and 35 days to metamorphosis and to start coloring up. Depending on the species.

Damsel Fish

There are many species that do well in a nano reef, here are three that are less aggressive and do well in small groups.

1. The Yellow Tail Damsel Fish (Chrysiptera parasema)
   These fish grow up to 2 ½ inches. They're a little aggressive and you should never keep just two unless they are a breeding pair. They are less aggressive than others in their genus. They're a hardy fish and up to six can be kept in a 15 to 20-gallon nano reef tank. They will eat most food offered and are good algae grazers. They do well with temperatures around 70 to 78 degrees.

2. Talbot's Damsel Fish (Chrysiptera talboti)
   The talkbots damsel fish grow up to about 3 inches and has a purplish pink and yellow head and a large spot under the dorsal fin. They're a little aggressive but less than many kinds of damsel

fish. They prefer a temperature between 70 to 78 degrees. They will eat most foods offered and graze on algae. Five would look nice in a 15 to 20-gallon nano reef.

3. The Allen's Damsel Fish (Pomacentrus alleni

These are known as the neon damsel fish. They're one of the less aggressive damsels. They're a planktivorous species. They have blue and yellow color and they grow up to 2 ½ inches. They will eat most foods offered. They prefer a temperature of 70 to 78 degrees and 6 will do well in a 15 to 20-gallon nano reef.

Clownfish (Amphiprioninae sp.)

Clownfish do well in a nano, they often will stake out small territories. There are three species that are small and a pair can be kept in as small as a 5-gallon nano reef. Ocellari's Clownfish (Amphiprion ocellaris), Percula Clownfish (Amphiprion percula), Pink Skunk Clownfish (Amphiprion perideraion). They all grow to around 2 ½ to 4 inches. Al captive bred, are hardy ad eat most food offered. The three mentioned are not overly aggressive like some species and can be kept with most companion fish or invertebrates with few problems. Their wild counterparts have close commonsel relationship with sea anemones. This is not mandatory in captivity but this is an entertaining relationship to watch. Most anemonies that a clownfish would use grow too large for nano like the bubbletip anemone (Entacmaea quadricolor), but the clownfish sometimes use substitutes like corals, sarcophyton leather corals. This can cause the polyps to stay closed but most become used to the presence of the clownfish. You can substitute a smaller maxi-mini anemone (Stichodactyla tapetum) or a rock flower anemone (Phymanthus crucifer) or a Condy anemone (Condylactis gigantea). These are commensal shrimp anemones. Ricordea also make good anemone substitute. They're a few other larger species of clownfish can be kept in a larger nano. A breeding pair or an individual in a 10 to 20-gallon reef tank like the tomato clownfish (Amphiprion frenatus) or the Maroon Clownfish (Premnas biaculeatus).

Bassletts

There are many diffifferent species of bassletts and most have beautiful colors and patterns. Most species are hardy, although there are some exceptions like anthias! They all do well with corals. Most bassletts prefer rock caves and overhangs. They generally eat most food offered.

Grammatidae

Grammas are beautiful fish and very hardy. The Royal Gramma (Gramma loreto) and the Black Cap Basslett (Gramma melacara), being the most popular. They grow to 3 or so inches. They are not to be trusted with ornamental shrimp although most invertebrates are fine. These two species are nest builders and use macro algae to build their nests in caves. Grammas lay their eggs individually and 20 to 260 eggs over the course of two weeks, mostly at night! The females are more rounded and the males are thinner and a little larger. The male royal gramma's pink portion is smaller. The fri are hatched at different times, usually at night so a fishtrap can collect them. The pelgagic fri can be fed large strain rotifers, brine shrimp nauplii, copepod nauplii and moina nauplii. Metamorphosis can take round 21 to 35 days. A brooding pair can be kept in a 10 to 15-gallon nano reef tank. They will eat most foods offered and they prefer a temperature of 70 to 78 degrees.

Dottybacks (Pseudochromis)

Dottybacks are beautiful and very aggressive, because of this they make good single fish for the nano tank. A breeding pair can be kept together if their large nano has smaller living area with a hole only the female can fit through and have access to the male's territory. Dottybacks can change sexes. The larger more dominant of the two will become the male. Dottybacks will eat most foods offered and are hardy. Their temperatures should be around 70 to 78 degrees. They can be kept with most invertebrates but shrimp and small crabs are not safe with them, although hermit crabs should be fine. Orchid Dottybacks (Pseudochromis fridmani) are less aggressive. The Neon Dottyback (Pseudochromis aldabraensis) are two of the most common species. Both grow to about 3 inches, all species have good personalities with their owners and are very outgoing. Many species have also been bred in captivity and are demersal spawners, laying their eggs on rock surfaces. The pelagic fri can be raised in a kreisel tank and fed small zooplankton. Most species metamorphosis around 25 to 35 days.

Liopropoma

These basslets have several interesting species like the Swiss guard basslets (Liopropoma carmabi). These are seen with some regularity, however the most beautiful and worthy of captive breeding are known as the Candy Bassletts (Liopropoma carmabi)! These deep water fish are hard to come by. Both species grow to around 3 inches. Their outgoing and can become personal with their owners. They do well with corals and most invertebrates. They are a little shy under bright lights but they will become eclamated over time. They fair better with caves and overhangs. They will eat most food offered and they prefer a temperature of 65 to 78 degrees. Liopropoma Basslets require a large breeder tank, at least 5 feet high and 3 feet wide. A plastic trash can will work. The reason such a large tank is required is their broadcast spawners. They will rise up into the water caluim and breed. Their fri are pro-larvae that are difficult to raise out of metamorphosis stage. The larvae feed on very small zooplankton.

Serranus Bassletts

Serranus Bassletts are hardy fish and are very personal with their owners. The Chalk Basslett (Serranus tortugarum), the Harlequin Basslett (Serranus tigrinus) and the Orange Back Basslett (Serranus annularis). They are all hardy and will eat most food offered. They all grow 3 to 4 inches and a pair or a trio in a 10 to 15-gallon nano reef will do fine.

Assessor Bassletts

Assessor Bassletts are small, around 2 inches, and have a peaceful nature. They do well with most invertebrates. They prefer caves and overhangs in their nano reef and can be kept in small groups or a pair in a 5-gallon nano reef. The Yellow Tail Assessor (Assessor flavissimus) and The Blue Fork Tail Assessor (Assessor macneilli). They will eat most food offered. Their temperature should be around 70 to 78 degrees. They are mouth brooders. The females are a little smaller and rounder and the males mouth brood the eggs. The pelagic fri can be raised in a kreisel tank and fed small zooplankton.

The Order of (Scorpaeniformes)

There are many species in the order of Scorpaniformes. There are 1400 species and 35 families and 300 genera. There are many that can be kept in a nano because of their sedetary nature and there are several smaller species. They prefer caves and overhangs. They do well with corals but they produce a lot of waste so sps corals are better left out of the tank. Because of their sit and ambush nature, they can smother corals by sitting on them. Pilar rocks with caves and overhangs can help prevent this. Most are good eaters and some may be intised over to frozen foods. They tend to do well in a larger nano reef tank. They also shed their skin or cuticle. Some species shed more often like the leaf's Scorpion Fish (Taenianotus Triacanthus). This species sheds twice a month but most do not and over shedding can be an indicator for poor health. For the most part, they are hardy fish. Many are mild to very poisonous and a sting can make you sick so use caution! Scorpion fish and Lion Fish usually lay a gelatinous blob or ribbon eggs. They have pelagic larvae fri that are difficult to raise passed metamorphosis and should be raised in a Kreisal tank. They can be fed micro zooplankton. To help induce breeding the pair can be introduced into a larger tank after increased feeding, lighting and a slight temperature change. They require a taller tank for spawning, they rise up in the water calium to copulate.

1. The Caribbean Reef Scorpionfish (Scorpaenodes caribbaeus)
    These little monsters grow up to 5 inches. Their very hardy and slow eaters but tend to eat well on live minnows but can be weaned over to frozen shrimp and minnows. They prefer a temperature of 65 to 78 degrees. Their head and fins are spotted; they have no tassels like so many scorpion fish do. They can be personable with their owners. They like caves and overhangs. One in a 15 to 20-gallon long nano reef tank will do well.

2. The Lowfin Coral Scorpionfish (Scorpaenodes parvippinnis)
    These little guys do well on the reef in a 15 to 20-gallon long nano tank. They are nocturnal and prefer a temperature of 70 to 78 degrees. They prefer live shrimp but can be weaned onto frozen foods.

3. The Yellow Spotted Scorpionfish (Sebastapistes cyanostigma)
    They are usually a brick-red and have yellow spots. They are more attractive than most scorpionfish and do well in a 15 to 20-gallon nano reef tank as a pair. In the wild they live in coral branches

and prefer a temperature of 70 to 78 degrees. They prefer live foods, shrimp and minnows but can be weaned over to frozen shrimp and minnows.

4. The Leaf Scorpionfish (Taenianotus triacanthus)
   The leaf scorpionfish are very charming. They grow up to 4 inches. Their more social scorpionfish. They have small mouths and prefer live foods but can be weaned onto frozen mysis as their main food source and their favorite food. They prefer a temperature of 70 to 78 degrees. Their very colorful and some of the most desirable are pinks, reds, yellows and combinations of these colors. They can lighten and darken these colors in accordance with their moods and environment.

5. The Waspfish (Ablabys sp.)
   These fish are similar to the leaf scorpionfish and have small mouths and prefer live mysis shrimp and may be weaned onto frozen foods. They prefer temperatures of 70 to 78 degrees and do well in a long nano reef tank of 15 to 20-gallons. The most commonly seen Cockatoofish (Ablabys taenianotus), they grow up to 6 inches and the Long Spined Waspfish (Paracentropogon longispinis).

Lionfish for the Nano Reef (Dendrochirus sp.)

There are only two species that I would recommend for the nano tank! The Fumanchu Lionfish (Dendrochirus biocellatus). They grow up to 5 inches and are the smallest Lionfish species and are solitary by nature. Their more inclined to crawl and hop across the bottom. They have attractive orange and black color and two whisker like appendages. They also have two black spots on their rear dorsal fin. They prefer live shrimp and minnows and are slow to change over to frozen foods. They should be fed two or three times a week. They are primarily nocturnal.

The Green Lionfish (Dendrochirus barberi)

This species grows up to 6 inches and are usually greenish color. They have red eyes. They also prefer to hop and slide across the bottom. They prefer shrimp or minnows and are easier to switch over to frozen foods. They are primarily nocturnal. Both species do fine in a 15 to 20-gallon long nano reef with caves and overhangs. They prefer a temperature of 68 to 78 degrees.

Lizardfish (Synodontidae sp.)

Lizardfish are carnivorous fish and shrimp predators and this makes them prime candidates for the nano reef. A pair can be kept together in a 15 to 20-gallon long tank. They prefer to burrow in the sand during the day and are primarily nocturnal. They like to jump so a screen lid may be necessary or a lower water level. They prefer a temperature of 68 to 78 degrees. Breeding the males form spawning territories and females will visit after dark and spawning may take place up to three times over the night. Their eggs and larvae are pelagic and difficult to raise. Small zooplankton may help raise them in a kreisel tank.

The Anglerfish (Antennariidae)

Anglerfish are very odd looking fish and have an unusual method of catching prey. Most have a lure that is called a esca. The esca moves and twitches or moves in a circular motion to attract prey. Some species esca looks like a worm and others, a shrimp or even a tiny fish. Anglerfish make interesting displays in a 15 or 20-gallon long nano reef with caves and dugouts will make them more at home. Anglerfish are not strong swimmers and prefer to walk across the bottom. They are also sensitive to bacteria and parasite infestation and need regular water changes. This will help reduce nitrates and infestations. Anglerfish are sit and wait ambush predators. They prefer live food like shrimp and minnows but can be enticed into frozen foods. Most do fine with a temperature of 68 to 78 degrees. There are many species to choose from, the warty frog fish is a good choice. They grow up to 4 inches and are mellow natured. Anglerfish spawn by rising up into the water calium and lay two different types of eggs ribbon or blobs. The pelagic fri are very small larvae with a lengthy pelagic stage and can take one or two months to metamorphosis. There are a few species like the tasselles anglerfish (Rhycherus filamentosus) that lay eggs with large fri that are easier to raise.

A Moray for the Nano

The Golden Dwarf Moray (Gymnothorax melatremus). I know what you are thinking, a moray in a nano. These species grow up to 7 to 10 inches and have a sedentary nature and can spend a lot of time with only their head sticking out of their cave. They will do well in a 15 to 20-gallon nano reef. They prefer shrimp and a fish on occasion and can be enticed over to frozen foods. There are a few more moray eels that can be kept in the nano; Chestnut Moray (Enchelycore carychoa) grows to 13 ½ inches, Herre's Moray eel (Gymnothorax herrei) grows to 12 inches, Richardson's Moray (Gymnothorax richardsonii) Richardson's Moray (Gymnothorax richardsonii) grows up to 13 inches, Brown Moray (Gymnothorax brunneus) grows up to 9 ¾ inches. Morays are broadcast spawners and rise into the water calcum to copulate and their fri are pro-larvae and can take a few months to metamorphosis and would be difficult to raise past metamorphosis and they would require a large and tall tank for successful spawning.

Chapter 7 Invertebrates

Invertebrates are an amazing group! Everything from tiny Boxing Crabs (Lybia sp.) waving their tiny pom pom anemones like pompoms to the great barrier reef that rivals the Sistine Chapel! They can feed mankind like shrimp farms or even the giant whales of the seas eat huge schools of krill. Invertebrates live in the sea and fly through the air. They are desert shrimp that can live for years with their vernal pools dried up in eggs that are what is called a ephippia stage or resting eggs and as soon as the rain comes, they hatch out and grow rapidly into adulthood and breed and lay eggs, sometimes in less than a month. Not all the eggs hatch at the same time, the reason is to ensure species survival so if the vernal pools dry up before the shrimp can breed and lay eggs, there are still eggs in the dry earth for next year. There are interesting inverts like Tardigrades. These too can live in a cocoon like state for up to 80 years and wake up like nothing has happened when the rains come. They have been tested with extreme cold and hot weather and radiation, in this suspended state and still lived. So invertebrates can be pretty amazing!

Octopus for the Nano!

The Caribbean Pygmy Octopus. Did you know there are octopus that can live in a nano? The Caribbean Pygmy Octopus (Octopus joubini/meratoris) grows just a few inches and are less cannibalistic than other octopus. They're much less interested in escaping their tanks like larger species and can be kept in small groups as long as they have their own caves. These Cephalopods are related to mollusk like snails and clams. They are nocturnal and can be viewed with night lights but will come out for feeding time on their own if you feed at the same time every day. They prefer small hermit crabs and small shrimp and can be weaned over to frozen mysis shrimp. Cophalopods are also very sensitive to copper! Octopus can get bored of their surroundings and some appreciate small toys or a mirror. The Caribbean Pygmy Octopus also lives in Florida and are often found in or under large shells or you can find local venders and they may ship them to you. The octopus unfortunately have short lives. They live only six months to a year and before octopus die, they go into a zombie like state called senescence. This happens after breeding. The males are usually the first to go into senescence and the females will live longer and lay eggs and care for them until they hatch and usually right after they too go into a state of senescence and die! They lay up to 50 larger eggs with no-pelagic stage. Baby octopus that can be fed small zooplankton like brine shrimp nauplii, copepods, moina and as they grow larger, small mysis shrimp and amphipods. The baby octopus should be kept in a separate larger tank with sand and stacks of plastic tubing or very small pvc pipes to hide in and reduce cannibalism. They need frequent water changes but no corals with the babies because they can eat them! Three can be kept in a 15 to 20-gallon long nano reef for sub adults and adults. The corals can't have aggressive stinging nematocyst!

Your octopus are best kept at cooler temperatures of 65 to 74 degrees. The reason is, higher temperatures can shorten their already short lives. There are other Pygmy Octopus like the Atlantic Pygmy Octopus (Octopus joubini), the Star-Sucker Pygmy Octopus (Octopus wolfi), the Disuet's Pygmy Octopus (Octopus digueti). There are also a few Pygmy Squid species that are rarely available. The Hawaiin Bobtail Squid (Euprymna scolopes) and the Southern Bobtail Squid (Euprymna tasmanica). These two species tend to spend a lot of time buried in the sand. They are ambush hunters. The other species worth mentioning is the Pygmy Squid (Idiosepius pygmaeus). These are very little guys! They top out at only 1 inch. They live in Tropical Asia in seagrass beds and maybe worth shipping back to the states. They have the unusual personality of a shrimp mimic. They settle and rest attached with a thread that they produce on the undersides of seagrass leaves and can dispatch instantly. These pygmy squid only live 100 days and have pelagic baby squid and could be raised on small zooplankton in a Kreisal tank! Cephalopods are amazing intelligent animals and worthy of of ower effort!

Starfish

There are a few species of starfish that can be kept in a nano reef tank with corals. Starfish can be introduced after the reef is established at least 3 months is recommended. This will give the reef time to completely cycle and start beneficial algae and micro fana. Starfish are sensitive to high nitrates. Starfish are sensitive to oxygen changes and copper based medicines. They prefer a temperature of 68 to 78 degrees.

Red Fromia (Fromia elegans)

These are one of the hardier fromias. They arrive on live rocks a little worse for ware and recover most of the time. Fromia stars are a very colorful genus. Their a little on the contacurus side. They require feeding once or twice a week and the starfish food should be places right in front of them.

Asterina Starfish (Asterina sp)

These are very small starfish about ¾ inch or less. They reproduce primarily through a-sexual reproduction and may also be brooding, starfish with no pelagic larvae. They are said to be coral eaters but it is in my finding that this almost never happens. There are some species of Asterina starfish that may eat coral, Asterina starfish are detritus feeders and they eat algae and fish foods. They're considered beneficial.

Red Thorny Starfish (Echinaster echinophorus)

These five arm starfish grow up to 3 inches and can be kept with corals with minimum problems. They eat sponges and algae and starfish food. They are red orange in color. They are found all over the Caribbean Sea. They can produce two types of eggs planktonic which are dark in color and those sink to the bottom are orange in color and hatch brachiolaria larva starfish. It is possible to raise them but this is difficult. My starfish food mix with sponges added may help.

The Spotted Linka Starfish (Linckia multifora)

This long arm starfish is multicolored spots red, white, orange or even blue. They grow 2 to 5 inches. They are from the Indian Ocean. They shed arms on occasion and these grow into new starfish also known as a-sexual reproduction and the starfish grows a new arm. They eat starfish food with sponges added and algae and bacteria. Some larger Linka starfish eat tridacna clams but the spotted Linka Starfish is less prone to this. They are reef safe with minimal problems. Keep your starfish fed, this will reduce problems!

Micro brittle Starfish

These tiny starfish reproduce rapidly through a-sexual reproduction. They require no care except for a healthy nano tank. They will eat discarded foods and nitrates and are nocturnal. Other small species of brittle and serpent starfish have the same care but should be fed a little food, overall their all easy and do great on their reef.

Sea Urchins

There are sea urchins that will do fine in the nano reef but urchins are ravenous algae eaters and will need to be fed. They eat sea urchin mix and this mostly consists of macro algae. Many also eat Coralline algae or zooxanthellae and this can be a problem. They sometimes graze on corals. The blue tuxedo urchins (Mespilia globulus) and the hairy pincushion sea urchin (Tripneustes gratilla). Both of these species grow around 3 inches and are less likely to eat Coralline algae. Sea Urchins are sensitive to copper based medicines. They also like to pick up objects and carry them around as camouflage and this also includes corals. So everything needs to be glued down or grown in place. This sea urchin species prefer temperatures of 68 to 78 degrees. They are fairly hardy and easy to care for.

Food Mix for Starfish and Sea Urchins

This food mix can be made with Macro Algae and various varieties and fish, mysis shrimp or grass shrimp, brine shrimp, moina, white worms or grindal worms, and sponge is recommended and multi vitamins and a mix of

HUFAs concentrate. Mix in a blender and lay flat in a tray and freeze. Then cut into small cubes. Starfish prefer a 50/50 mix and sea urchins prefer a 75/25 mostly greens. These mixes are also great for spawning angelfish.

Shrimp for the Nano Reef

Shrimp are ideal for the nano reef. Their small and don't produce much waste and they only need food two or three times a week. There are many ornamental shrimp species to choose from. They can be kept with many different species of corals and some have commensal relationships with anemones. Most can be kept in very small nano reef tanks. Shrimp are very entertaining to watch with a personality of their own.

Sexy Shrimp (Thor amboinensis)

These shrimp are tiny one inch or less. They are active by day, shaking their bodies around and they have commensal relationships with anemones and do well with dwarf seahorses and small gobies. They can be kept in small groups. The males are smaller and the females have a broken band across their back and tail. They will eat most food offered and nibble coral slime a little. Their temperature should be 70 to 78 degrees. They have been bred and their larvae can be raised in a kreisel tank. They can be fed brine shrimp nauplii, copepod nauplii and moina nauplii from the start. These are pretty shrimp and do well in even a two gallon nano reef.

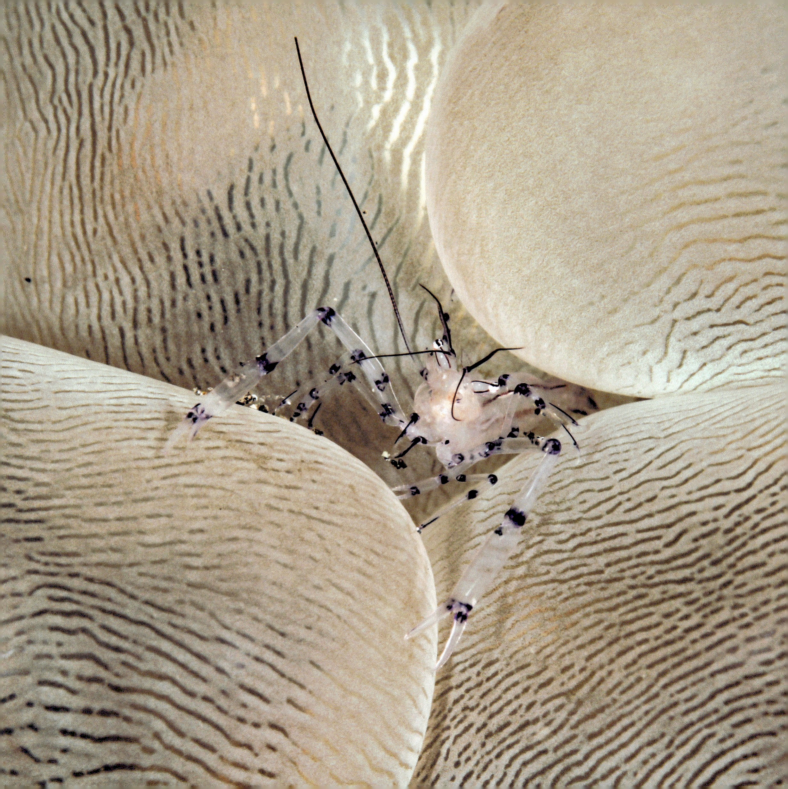

Periclimenes Shrimp

These shrimp are also about one inch and are beautifully colored with blue and white with clear bodies. They have a commensal relationship with anemones and do well with corals and eat little slime from them. They can be fed most kinds of food and can be kept with dwarf seahorses and small gobies. They can be bred in the same manner as sexy shrimp and larvae care is the same way. They prefer a temperature of 70 to 78 degrees. They can be kept in small groups in as small as a two gallon nano reef.

Pistol Shrimp (Alpheus sp.)

These shrimp have a close relationship with shrimp gobies. They can live in the shrimp's tunnel and the gobies lets the almost blind shrimp no when danger is nearby! They safely retreat into the shrimp cave tunnel. Not all pistol shrimp species have a commensal relationship with gobies and some grow large and may eat gobies! Make sure you know your species. However, the ones that do are more outgoing. Many pistol shrimp are colorful and have one large claw that can snap shut at 62 miles per hour and stun predators and prey. They will eat most food offered and prefer a temperature of 70 to 78 degrees.

Lysmata Shrimp

These are perhaps the most popular shrimp species kept. They are all colorful and hardy will eat most foods offered. They do well with many different fish species. They're a little larger and less likely to be harmed. They can be kept with most corals including sps and lps corals but no anemones unless their maxi mini (Stichodactyla Tapetum) because they may eat them. They fair better in a 15 to 20-gallon nano reef and most are outgoing most of the time. They are cleaner shrimp and may clean fish in the nano tank and all are sensitive to rapid water changes.

The Skunk Shrimp

There are two species, one from the Pacific Ocean (Lysmata amboinensis) and the other from the Atlantic Ocean (Lysmata grabhami). Both look almost identical. These shrimp are out in the open most of the time searching for food. Sometimes they may retreat to a shadowy overhang. They do well in groups and can be bred and raised in a kreisel tank. Check live food culture on Lysmata for larvae care and culture.

The Blood Shrimp (Lysmata debelius)

These shrimp are beautifully colored deep red with patches of white. They are a little shy, more than the Skunk Shrimp, and are primarily nocturnal. They hang out under shadowy overhangs and caves. They too can be captive bred and the larvae raised in a kreisel tank. They are a little more solitary by nature.

The Peppermint Shrimp (Lysmata wurdemanni)

These shrimp are a little smaller and are not as flashy as the first two but still pretty! They are primarily nocturnal and prefer shadowy overhangs and caves. They are very social and can be kept in groups. They are more cannibalistic especially during molting. They can be bred like other Lysmata shrimp and do so often, but their larvae are smaller than other Lysmata and a little more difficult to raise.

The Boxing Shrimp (Stenopus hispidus)

These semi aggressive shrimp are great with larger fish and are cleaner shrimp, but may prey on smaller fish. They do well single or in mater pairs. The males are usually smaller. Use caution if they don't pair up they may fight to the death. They have red and white bands and are pretty. They can grow around 3 inches and a little over 6 inches with their antenna. Boxing shrimp are carnivorous and will eat most foods offered including pellets and flake foods. They are a hardy shrimp but sensitive to copper and high nitrates. Iodine helps them molt their exo-skeleton. Other species also are great reef buddies. The banded coral blue shrimp (S. tenuirostris). This colorful little shrimp is a little more peaceful and colorful red, blue, white and yellow in color. They grow about 1 ½ inches but up to 3 inches with their antennas. The gold banded coral shrimp (S. zanzibaricus), they grow around 2 ½ inches but up to 5 inches with their antennas. Their colors are yellow, red and white. These two species care are the same as the Boxing Shrimp.

Crabs for the Nano Reef

There are a few crabs that do well in the nano reef. They will eat detritus, discarded fish foods and algae and can be beneficial to the reef in this way. However, all crabs are predatory by nature at least to some degree and very small species are recommended. They prefer a temperature of 68 to 78 degrees.

The Boxing Crab (Lybia tessellata)

These pretty little crabs have an entertaining behavior. They carry around two tiny anemones in their claws and wave them like pom poms at any predator for protection. When the crabs molt they set their anemones down and when molting is complete, they pick them back up and go about their crabby business. This commensal relationship also benefits the anemones. When the crab eats, they are fed cast of foods. They do well in nanos and are hardy but their anemones are a little more delicate and may grow throughout the tank.

The Porcelain Crabs (Neopetrolisthes sp.)

These little crabs have a commensal relationship with anemones. They will do well with small anemones like rose (Epicystis Ctucifer) or flower rock Anemone (Stichodactyla tapetum). They will do fine with replacements like ricordia. They usually eat what their anemones feed on but will accept most food offered and probably nibble on slime from their host. They define the definition of a nano reef and are a little delicate and drop their claws if handled.

Trapezia Crabs (Trapezia wardi)

These pretty crabs are coral crabs. They spend most of their lives on sps coral branches but can adapt to other corals. They sometimes will snip off coral to nibble on but if they are fed this rarely occurs. They will eat most foods offered. They are territorial and will defend their corals. They do well in a nano reef. Two or three in a 10-gallon tank will do fine and stake out little territory of their own.

Hermit Crabs

There are several different hermit crab species that are small and mostly eat algae and lost fish foods. They will eat most foods offered. They do have a bad habit of eating snails and stealing their shells. They do well in a nano reef and here are a few more commonly kept species and will need extra shells. The Blue Legged Hermit Crab (Clibanarius tricolor), they grow about 1 inch. They Scarlet Hermit Crab (Paguristes cadenati), they grow a little larger than 1 inch. The Blue Knuckle Hermit Crab (Calcinus elegans), they grow to about 2 inches. Less common The Orange Striped Hermit Crab (Ciliopagurus strigatus), they have flat bodies and use cone snail shells. They prefer a more carnivorous diet and grow up to 2 inches.

Snails and Seahares

These companions for the nano reef are great nuisance algae and detritus eaters and are beneficial. They can be kept in any size nano with supplemental feeding on occasion.

Nerite Snails (Neritina sp.)

These are usually hardy and have pretty shells. They sometimes have the bad habit of crawling out of the tank. They eat algae but are more detritus feeders. They grow about 1 ½ inches.

Turbo Snails (Astraea sp.) (Lithopoma sp.)

These are the best algae grazers of most any snail. They will make short work of most algae infestation. They are hardy and do well but if they flip over on the sand, they have trouble reriting themselves and may die! They may require an occasional macro algae feeding or may eat spirulina as a substitute. They grow about 1 1/8 inches.

Cerith Snails (Cerithium sp.)

These have a waffle cone shaped shell. These are hardy snails and do eat algae but are a little more inclined to eat fish food and detritus. They grow less than 1 inch.

There are a few seahares that can be kept in the nano reef. Any can be kept in the nano when small but some grow up to 10 inches. Here are a few that stay a moderate size; (Aplysia parvula) and (Bursatella sp) seahares can be great algae and detritus eaters and can be supplemented with spirulina and macro algae. Some species like (Bursatella sp) will eat Cyanobacteria. Seahares can release a non-toxic purple ink when disturbed. This is similar to cephalopod ink but does not appear to be toxic, a large water change is required. You need to cover the intake with a screen, the filter will chop them up!

The Lettuce Sea Slug (Elysia sp.)

These beautiful slugs are also great algae eaters and can be supplemented with macro algae. They use chloroplasts in their tissue from the algae and need light and algae to thrive. Their lighting needs to be 6500 to 1200K. They do well in a nano reef tank but you need to cover the intake with a screen.

Giant Clams (Tridacna sp.) and (Hippopus sp.)

Giant clams are great additions to the nano reef and even though all but T.crocea will have to be removed after a few years, they are beneficial to filtration and protein intake. Their mantiles come in many colors and patterns. There is no reef complete without them.

Tridacna crocea

This is the smallest species and grows to about 6 inches. They're a shallow sea species. They require bright lighting of 6500k to 1200k in order to thrive. They are often shipped without their anchor mantle and may have difficulty settling in posterior position because of their high lighting demands. They have high lighting demands and do well with sps and lps corals. They're one of the least dependent giant clams on nutrition export from the water. They require high calcium levels and are quick to deplete this resource. They need a healthy system in order to thrive and are very tolerant of salinity changes. They are one of the most beautiful of the giant clams!

Tridacna maxima

This is a larger species but with similar care requirements as T. crocea. They are often found in a little deeper water and don't require quite as bright of lighting. They require high calcium levels and are quick to deplete this resource. These are very beneficial clams and are variable in color and pattern. They do well with sps and lps corals and a 10 to 20-gallon reef can be their home for a few years.

Tridacna squamosa

This is a larger species and pretty. They can be kept for a few years at a small size in a larger nano. Their more adaptive to dimmer lighting or at the bottom of the tank. Their also great at nutrition export and remove huge amounts of proteins and plankton from the water and when their removed from the tank, there is often a noticeable increase in algae. They require high calcium levels and will deplete this resource quickly. They do well with corals and are beneficial.

Hippopus sp.

These Giant clams are one of the easiest. They require moderate lighting and do well with 20.000k. This species is often found in heavy sediment and is very adept to filter feeding. They too remove huge amounts of proteins and nutrions from the water and are beneficial. They have smaller mantle lips than Tridacna sp. They are often a greenish color and are pretty. They require high calcium demands and will deplete this resource rapidly. They do well in a larger nano reef at least for a few years.

Chapter 8   Corals

About 80% of all life on planet earth comes from the world's oceans. There are thought to be 70,000 species of corals in the world. Do to climate change and rise in temperature and pollution, large areas of the world's stoney corals have started to die off. This is called coral bleaching. Some places recover due to stronger strains of zooxanthellae or coralline algae that are more resistant to increasing temperatures. Most corals are colonial and have connected polyps that feed a single hive. Corals are all from the class of Anthozoa within the phylum of cnidarian anthozoa in greek words means flower animals. All corals capture prey in their tentacles and most eat zooplankton, even corals that grow zooxanthellae in their tissue. Some corals feed on larger prey like shrimp and even small fish with their stinging nematocyst. Sea anemones and jellyfish are related to corals. Corals are over 500 million years old and existed during the Paleozoic era. Corals really are a beautiful diverse ecosystem and there's nothing like walking into your home and seeing this miniature world.

Corals Planula Larvae

The Difference Between Ciliated and Non-Ciliated Larvae

1. Ciliated
   These are called gonochorism or have separate sexes. Males shed sperm into the water and the female corals absorb the sperm through the mouth of the polyp through internal fertilization of the eggs. Brooding corals grow well developed eggs and the planula larvae. These planulae may settle after one day sometimes around the base of the parent colony or drift in the current for a few days or a week or so before settling. The zygote will develop into a planula larva after fertilization. As the polyp drift and begins to settle in a suitable location. The polyp has what is called surface control over the location where it settles. This location is usually permanent and after the planula settles, it goes through metamorphosis and changes into a polyp. The polyp filter feeds through its mouth zooxanthellae or coralline algae of that species choice and then the

polyp will a-sexually reproduce and continue to do so until a new colony is born. Ciliated corals will usually reproduce throughout most of the year.

2. Seasonal Reproduction

    Seasonal reproduction is usually in accordance with the timing of lunar or moon cycle and light and dark regime. They reproduce during winter and temperature likely plays effect. Coral reproduction also has to do with geographic region or variation within a species in different geographic location. This is called synchronicity and many corals will only reproduce during these times on particular locations, usually after sunset. These types of corals are known as the broadcast spawners. About ¾ of all zooxanthellae corals are hermaphrodites or broadcast spawners and they release thousands or millions of eggs.

3. Non-Ciliated Larva

    These coral colonies are hermaphrodite and their reproductive organs are inside the body cavity and lie on the mesentery or septa. Hermaphrodite colonies shed sperm and eggs into the water column and the eggs drift for a month or two. These corals are known as broadcast spawners and the longer they drift in the current, the planula use surface control over selecting a suitable usually permanent location. The planula settle and metamorphosis into a polyp. The polyp will feed on zooxanthellae or coralline algae and begin to a-sexually reproduce and this is how a new coral colony is born.

4. Hybridization

    Hybridization can occur in the wild due to synchronicity in different coral species and with some regularity. The hybrid corals can look similar to their species but have a different genetic composition However, most corals reproduce in their own species or there would be only one species of coral in the world!

Breeding Brooding Ciliated Corals in the Nano

Brooding coral can be bred in captivity. Some breed on their own and some can be manipulated to breed in a nano reef tank. By extending then shortening there light cycle and by extending and reducing the temperature over and extended period of time. This with a night light that increases and decreases the luner cycle and zooplankton feeding, may help to breed your corals in the nano reef tank or a separate small 10 to 20-gallon tank with the same species can be manipulated to spawn. Adding a little breeding hormone to the water may help after conditioning the corals.

Coral Planula Larva Care

This usually consists of a large kreisel or plastic circular container and let the coral planula drift in the current. Use small pieces of live rock with coralline algae or zooxanthellae from the parent coral's tank and the planula will settle and metamorphosis into polyps. The coral polyp will feed on coralline algae and absorb the species of that coral's choosing and the polyp will a-sexually reproduce new polyps. During this time, feed the polyps small zooplankton. Some will grow and start new colonies. Some species that can be bred in the nano tank; sun corals (Tubastraea sp.), Plate Corals (Fungia Sp.).

Large seafans, sea plumes and sea whips (Gorgonacea sp.) may need a large tank for spawning. There are other species, 25% of zooxanthellae corals reproduce cilated larva and are brooding corals. Many temperate water corals and anemones reproduce sexually this way.

Zoanthids

There are three different orders of Zoanthids. The Palythoa sp, Protopalythoa sp, and Zoanithus sp. The first two are very similar in appearance. Protopalythoa sp have separate polyps connected to a base of coenenchyme and Palythoa Sp are connected to each other. They are both erect and up to one inch wide polyps. Zoanthus have a shorter, more compact polyps and easy to identify. Most species of zoanthids are colorful and beautiful patterns. They resemble a garden of flowers. Zoanthids are a beginner coral and do well in almost any nano reef. They prefer moderate to rapid water flow and medium to bright light. They are a little more tolerant of nitrates and are a non-aggressive soft coral.

Mushroom Corals

Mushroom corals are very beautiful and look similar to anemones. There are several different species, all do well in a nano reef and are beginner corals. They do well with low to moderate water flow and moderate to bright light. They reproduce a-sexually, often this is called budding. Temperature should be 68 to 78 degrees.

Discosoma sp.

Most Discosma sp have smoother polyps. However, there are a few exceptions like the Saint Thomas Mushroom Corals (Discosoma sanctithomae). They have bubble tenticles. Some Discomas can produce a mild chemical that can inhabit the growth of some stony corals. They bud and reproduce fairly quickly a-sexually. They are very hardy.

Rhodactis sp.

These have a rougher bumber polyps. Some can produce a mild chemical that can inhibit the growth of some Stony corals. They bud and reproduce fairly quickly a-sexually and are very hardy soft corals. Rhodactus usually has larger polyps than discosoma. They can reproduce farliy quickly through a-sexual budding. They are very hardy.

Ricordea sp.

They look the most like bubble tip anemones. They are very hardy. They reproduce a-sexually budding but this is slower than the other two species. They are also more tolerant of more rapid water flow.

Density 1.021 to 1.026	Stronium
PH 7.9 to 8.2	Iron 0.1 to 0.3 ppm
Calcium	Iodine 0.05 to 0.08 ppm
Magnesium	Silicates 0.05 ppm

Octo Corals

These soft corals have eight tentacles to a polyp. This group includes xenia, clavularia, seapens, gorgonians and more. They are an interesting group. Some can move like xenia, or clavularia and can come in many colors and forms. Most are easy to care for and do well in the nano reef tank.

Ammonia 0.00 ppm	Nitrate 0.25 ppm
Nitrate 0.00 ppm	They will tolerate this for a short time

Xenia sp.

These octocorals are beautiful and one of the only moving and pulsing soft corals and it is said that they capture zooplankton in this way. They grow with zooxanthellae or coralline algae in their tissue and can reproduce rapidly under moderate to bright lights. They also seem to benefit from iodine added to their reef and may begin pulsing more rapidly. Xenia prefer moderately rapid water flow and can slide to a more desireable location similar to a sea anemone but they will lose pieces of their base and these will polyp up and grow new xenias. They have been known to crash and melt away for no apparent reason so they are recommended for the intermediate beginner. Temperature should be 68 to 78 degrees. They are a non-aggressive soft coral.

Density 1.021 to 1.026	Iodine 0.05 to 0.08 ppm
PH 7.9 to 8.2	Phosphate 0.05 ppm
Calcium 300 ppm	Silicate 0.05 ppm
Magnesium 1100 ppm	Nitrate up to 10.0 ppm
Stronium 7.0 to 10.0 ppm	Nitrate 0.00 ppm
Iron 0.05 to 0.07 ppm	Ammonia 0.00 ppm

Xenia may also benefit from trace elements.

Sympodium sp.

These very attractive blue and green octicorals are in the family of Xeniidae. Their a hardy and adaptive coral. They prefer to be placed lower in the nano tank and do well with moderate water flow. They do well under moderate lighting and a temperature of 68 to 78 degrees. They can be kept at the same water chemistry as Xenia sp. They are a non-aggressive soft coral.

Clove Polyps (Clavularia sp.)

These octi-corals are encrusting and grow on a coenenchyme base. They are a hardy soft coral and a good starter species. They seem to from occasional zooplankton feeding but grow coralline algae in their tissue. They do well under moderate lighting and moderate water flow. They can be placed at any level in the nano reef and are non-aggressive. Temperature should be 68 to 78 degrees.

Density 1.021 to 1.026	Iodine 0.05 to 008 ppm
PH 7.9 to 8.2	Silicate up to 0.05 ppm
Calcium 350 to 400 ppm	Phosphate up to 0.05 ppm
Magnesium 1100 to 1300 ppm	Nitrates up to 10.0 ppm
Stronium 7.0 to 10 ppm	Nitrate 0.00 ppm
Iron 0.1 to 0.3 ppm	Ammonia 0.00 ppm

They seem to benefit from trace elements.

Jasmine Coral Polps (Knopia sp.)

These hardy beautiful octi-corals colors are usually pink, green or brownish with white. They are a beginner soft coral and seem to benefit from occasional zooplankton feeding but have coralline algae in their tissue and receive most of their food energy from this. They are mildly aggressive and are best placed near the bottom of the nano reef. They do well with moderate water flow and moderate lighting. Their water chemistry is the same as Clavularia sp.

Organpipe Coral (Tubipora musica)

These octi-corals are peaceful and have a calcareous base called a coenenchyme. They do well under lighting and moderate water flow. They can be placed anywhere in the nano reef. They seem to benefit from occasional zooplankton feeding. Their water chemistry is the same as Clavularia sp.

Gorgonacea

The seafans, seaplumes and seawhips are a fascinating genus and are very common corals throughout the Caribbean Sea but can be found throughout the world's oceans. Many species are without zooxanthellae and difficult to keep and are better left in the sea. However many species of gorgonian have coralline algae in their tissue and are photosynthesizing and can be kept. Some gorgonans are little sensitive and will not tolerate high nitrates. Photosynthesizing gorgonans are also zooplankton feeders and do better with regular feedings. If your gorgorans grow too large for your nano, they can be trimmed and cut. The cut pieces can be fraged and put on plugs to start a new colony. The best way to tell photosynthesizing gorgonans in most have brownish or tan polyps. Some are creamy light color and barely disernable and difficult to tell apart but experience will help you tell them apart over time. The non-photosynthesizing gorgonians for the most part have white polyps but some have blue or red polyps. The skeleton or halaxonia also known as gorgonin. They are made up of keratin or a complete protein and also this contains iodine and bromine. They also have separate sexes and have ciliated larvae. Gorgonians do best under moderately bright lighting around 10,000k to 20,000k. They do best under rapid water flow. They are a peaceful coral. Under the wrong lighting, they are commonly overgrown with algae.

Temperature 60 to 78 degrees	
Density 1.021 to 1.026	Iodine 0.05 to 0.08 ppm
Ph 7.9 to 8.2	Silicate up to 0.05 ppm
Calcium 400.0 to 450.0 ppm	Phosphate up to 0.05 ppm
Magnesium 1100 to 1300 ppm	Nitrate up to 0.05 ppm
Stronium 7.0 to 10.0 ppm	Nitrate 0.00 ppm
Iron 0.1 to 0.3 ppm	Ammonia 0.00 ppm

They seem to benefit from trace elements.

Quill Gorgonian (Muricea laxa)

These gorgonians grow bushy. Their colors are usually a silver greenish and they have a bumpy texture. They have small polyps that are expanded throughout the day. They prefer a lower lighting and stronger water flow. They seem to benefit from zooplankton feedings but grow zooxanthellae in their tissue and photosynthesize. They are a peaceful coral.

Purple Candelabra Gorgonian (Antillogorgia bipinnata)

These are fast growing seafan and one of the easier gorgonians. They need moderately bright light and rapid water flow. They seem to benefit from regular zooplankton feedings but grow zooxanthellae in their tissue and are photosynthesizing. coral. They are peaceful corals.

Leather Corals (Alcyoniidae)

This attractive genus comes in many shapes and sizes! They have a leathery surface that they will shed periodically. This skin is mucus like and may come off in pieces their skin is mildly toxic. The corals polyps may stay closed for up to two weeks pre shed. Leather corals reproduce a-seually. They grow rapidly and will need trimming on occasion. These cut pieces can be fraged and put on plugs and you can start a new colony this way. They do well under moderately bright light and moderate water flow. Their temperature should be 68 to 78 degrees. They are mildly aggressive soft corals.

	Ph 7.9 to 8.2
Density 1.021 to 1.026	Phosphate up to 0.05 ppm
Calcium 350.0 ppm	Silicate up to 0.05 ppm
Magnesium 1100 ppm	Nitrate up to 0.15 ppm for a short time
Iron 0.1 to 0.3 ppm	Nitrate 0.00 ppm
Iodine 0.05 to 0.08 ppm	Ammonia 0.00 ppm

They seem to benefit from trace elements.

Sarcophyton sp.

These are known as toad stool leather corals. They can grow very large but can be trimmed to size in your nano and because of this, they do best in larger nano reefs. Their colors are usually browns, pinks, greens and yellows. They are hardy and mildly aggressive soft corals.

Lobophytum sp.

These are known as the devil's hand corals. They are a hardy and encrusting leather coral with branches rising from the base. They have off white polyps and come in a few colors, pinks, grays, browns and greens. They do well in large nano reefs.

Sinularia sp.

These leather corals have many species that go by many names; spaghetti, finger and cabage. They are all hardy and if trimmed, do well in most nano reefs. Sinularas come in many colors and are pretty, some of these are whites, greens, pinks, purples, greys, browns and beige.

Nephthea sp.

These beautiful corals are commonly called the cauliflower coral. Their colors are usually greens, purples, tans and yellows. Nephtheas are hard to identify on a species level because of their diversity and variation of individuals in a single species. These soft corals seem to benefit from occasional zooplankton feedings but they grow zooxanthellae in their tissue and are photosynthesis. They are semi-aggressive soft corals and produce mild toxic slime coat! They are a fairly easy coral to care for and prefer moderately bright lighting and moderate water flow. Their temperature should be 68 to 78 degrees.

Density 1.021 to 1.026	Silicate up to 0.05 ppm
Ph 7.9 to 8.2	Phosphate up to 0.05 ppm
Calcium 350.00 ppm	Nitrate up to 10.0 ppm
Magnesium	Nitrate 0.00 ppm
Stronium	Ammonia 0.00 ppm
Iodine 0.05 to 0.08 ppm	Iron 0.1 to 0.3 ppm

They seem to benefit from trace elements.

The Cornation Corals (Stereonephthya sp.)

These are a photosynthesizing species that grow zooxanthellae in their tissue. Not the non-photosynetic carnation corals. Their care is similar to Nephthea sp. They do well under moderate lighting and moderate water flow. They're non-aggressive soft corals. Their colors cn be reds, oranges and purples.

Capnella sp. (Family of Nephtheidae)

These soft corals are somewhat aggressive with chemical warfare. Most are easy to care for. They grow zooxanthellae in their tissue and are photosynthesizing. They do well under moderately strong lighting and moderately strong water flow. They should be placed in the mid to bottom level in the nano reef tank. Their temperature should be 68 to 78 degrees. Their water chemistry is the same as Nephthea.

Klyxum sp. Colt Corals (Cladiella genus)

These mildly aggressive soft corals use chemical warfare. They're an easy soft coral to care for and do best under moderately bright lighting. They need moderate water flow and can be placed anywhere in the nano reef. They seem to benefit from occasional zooplankton feedings. They grow zooxanthellae in their tissue and are photosynthesizing soft corals. They prefer a temperature of 68 to 78 degrees.

Density 1.021 to 1.026	Silicate up to 0.05 ppm
Ph 7.9 to 8.2	Phosphate up to 0.05 ppm
Calcium 350.0 ppm	Nitrate up to 0.10 ppm
Magnesium	Nitrate 0.00 ppm
Stronium	Ammonia 0.00 ppm
Iodine 0.05 to 0.08 ppm	Iron 0.1 to 0.3 ppm

They seem to benefit from trace elements.

Large Polyp Stony Corals

Lps corals are a diverse group. They're easier to care for then sps corals and most are less light demanding and more forgiving of water quality. Many species like to be fed supplement zooplankton, fish chunks or shrimp but most of the species we keep are photosynthesizing and grow coralline algae in their tissue for food. Lps corals grow tissue over a stony skeleton. Many of the lps corals are very beautiful and do well in a nano reef tank.

Sun Corals (Tubastraea sp.)

Sun corals are non-photosynthesizing. This means they have no zooxanthellae in their tissue. They require up to four feedings a week. They will eat zooplankton, worms, shredded fish pieces and even fish food flakes or pellets. Sun corals usually eat after dark but can be inticed to feed during the day, but use caution with small fish, they may eat them! There are about a half a dozen species and some can be difficult like the black sun coral (Tubastraea microanthus). Some are less difficult like (Tubastracea faulkneri), the most popular. They can be kept under low lighting but do best in a cave overhang. They do best with high calcium levels. They reproduce sexually and a-sexually. Planula larva often start new colonies in the nano reef. Their temperature should be 62 to 78 degrees and they prefer a more direct water flow.

Density 1.021 to 1.026	Iodine 0.005 to 0.08 ppm
Ph 7.8 to 8.2	Iron 0.1 to 0.3 ppm
Calcium 400.0 to 450.0 ppm	Silcate up to 0.05 ppm
Magnesium 1100 to 1300 ppm	Phosphate up to 0.05 ppm
Stronium 7.0 to 10.0 ppm	Nitrates up to 10.0 ppm
Nitrite 0.00 ppm	Ammonia 0.00 ppm

They seem to benefit from trace elements.

Favia sp. Favites sp. (Family faviidae)

These lps corals are easy to care for in a nano reef tank. They are semi-aggressive corals. They come in many different colors. They best way to tell the difference between the two is to examine their corallites. The individual corallites of favia are more raised and uneven in pattern and favites share a common wall similar to a honey comb. They grow zooxanthellae in their tissue and are photosynthesizing. They seem to benefit from zooplankton feedings on occasion. They do best under moderately bright lights and moderate water flow. Their temperature should be 68 to 78 degrees.

Density 1.021 to 1.026	
Ph 7.9 to 8.2	Silacate up to 0.05 ppm
Calcium 400.0 to 450.0 ppm	Phosphate up to 0.05 ppm
Magnesium 1100 to 1300 ppm	Nitrate up to 10.0 ppm
Stronium 7.0 to 10.0 ppm	Nitrite 0.00 ppm
Iodine 0.05 to 0.08 ppm	Ammonia 0.00 ppm
Iron 0.1 to 0.3 ppm	

They seem to benefit from trace elements.

The Autralian Acan Corals (Acanthastrea sp.)

These lps Stony Corals come in a range of colors and patterns and usually two or three color patterns on a single polyp. These semi-aggressive corals are easy to care for. They do well in any nano reef and do well closer to the bottom. They do best under moderately bright lights and moderate water flow. They grow zooxanthellae in their tissue and are photosynthesizing but they seem to benefit from occasional zooplankton feedings. Their temperature should be 68 to 78 degrees.

Density 1.021 to 1.026	Silicate up to 0.05 ppm
Ph 7.9 to 8.2	Phosphate up to 0.005 ppm
Calcium 400.0 to 450.0 ppm	Nitrate up to 0.10 ppm
Magnesium 1100 to 1300 ppm	Nitrite 0.00 ppm
Stronium 7.0 to 10.0 ppm	Ammonia 0.00 ppm
Iron 0.1 to 0.3 ppm	Iodine 0.05 to 0.08 ppm

They seem to benefit from trace elements.

Duncan Corals (Duncanopsammia axifuga)

The Duncan corals are pretty non-aggressive coral. Their colors range from brown and green combination or green and the most colorful florescent green and purple. They are a peaceful coral. They grow zooxanthellae in their tissue and photosynthesizing. They seem to benefit from zooplankton feedings. They prefer moderate lighting and a moderate water flow. They do well in any nano reef and prefer a temperature of 68 to 78 degrees. They are a good starter species into lps Corals.

Density 1.021 to 0.026	Silicate up to 0.05 ppm
Ph 7.9 to 8.2	Phosphate up to 0.05 ppm
Calcium 400.0 to 450.0 ppm	Nitrate up to 10.0 ppm
Magnesium 1100 to 1300 ppm	Nitrite 0.00 ppm
Stronium 7.0 to 10.0 ppm	Ammonia 0.00 ppm
Iodine 0.05 to 0.08 ppm	Iron 0.01 to 0.03 ppm

They seem to benefit from trace elements.

Trumpet Coral (Caulastraea sp.)

Caulastrea are one of the easiest lps corals. They range in color; brown, greens and blueish or combination of these colors. They do well under moderate lighting and moderate water flow. They usually reproduce a-sexually through budding polyps. There are at least three known species; C. furcata, being the most common, C. curvata and C. echinulata. There is still some debate that it's just one species, C. furcata. They should be maintained at a temperature of 68 to 78 degrees.

Density 1.021 to 1.026	Magnesium 1100 to 1200 ppm
Ph 7.9 to 8.2	Stronium
Calcium 400.0 to 450.0 ppm	Iodine 0.05 to 0.08 ppm
Iron 0.1 to 0.3 ppm	Nitrate up to 10.0 ppm
Silicate up to 0.05 ppm	Nitrite 0.00 ppm
Phosphate up to 0.05 ppm	Ammonia 0.00 ppm

They seem to benefit from trace elements.

Donut Coral (Scolymia sp.) Family Mussidae

Scolymia are solitary polyps. They reproduce a-sexually more commonly in the aquarium and will bud their polyp off the main polyp. They're very colorful usually florescent colors green and red-orange. The photo synthesizes by growing zooxanthellae in their tissue. They seem to benefit from zooplankton feedings. Their surface has a much smoother texture than Cynarina sp. There are currently five specie in the genus, the two most common are S. Australis and S. vitiensis. The last three are S. cubensis, S. lacarea and S. wellsii. They do best under moderately bright light and moderate water flow. They can be placed on rocks close to the bottom. They prefer a temperature of 68 to 78 degrees. These are mildly aggressive corals.

Density 1.021 to 1.026	Silicate up to 0.05 ppm
Ph 7.9 to 8.2	Phosphate up to 0.005 ppm
Calcium 400.0 to 450.0 ppm	Nitrate up to 10.0 ppm
Magnesium 1100 to 1300 ppm	Nitrite 0.00 ppm
Stronium 7.0 to 10.0 ppm	Ammonia 0.00 ppm
Iron 0.1 to 0.3 ppm iodine 0.05 to 0.08 ppm	

They seem to benefit from trace elements.

Botton Corals (Cynarina sp.) Mussidae Family

Cynarina are single polyp lps corals. Their colors usually are brownish or pink but a nice green color is seen on occasion and they have rippled polyps. They are an easy Lps starter coral and an be placed on a rock close to the bottom. They grow zooxanthellae in their tissue and are photosynthesizing corals. They prefer moderate lighting and moderate water flow. They can be fed zooplankton on occasion. Their temperature should be 68 to 78 degrees. The water chemistry is the same as Scolymia sp. They are mildly aggressive corals.

Blastomussa wellsi

These lps corals are a fairly easy species. They seem to do well closer to the bottom. They grow zooxanthellae in their tissue and are photosynthesizing but seem to benefit from occasional feeding of zooplankton. They're a peaceful species. They prefer moderate lighting and moderate water flow. Their temperature should be 68 to 78 degrees.

Density 1.021 to 1.026	Silicate up to 0.05 ppm
Ph 7.9 to 8.2	Phosphate up to 0.005 ppm

Calcium 400.0 to 450.0 ppm	Nitrate up to 10.0 ppm
Magnesium 1100 to 1300 ppm	Nitrite 0.00 ppm
Stronium 7.0 to 10.0 ppm	Ammonia 0.00 ppm
Iron 0.1 to 0.3 ppm	Iodine 0.05 to 0.08 ppm

They seem to benefit from trace elements.

Plate Corals (Fungia sp.)

Plate corals are one of the easier lps corals. They come in many different colors or companions of colors. The most common are greens, purples or reds. They prefer life on the sands and are capable of walking slowly across the sand on ciliary hairs or they inflate their bodies and pull themselves across the bottom If they are flipped over or buried, like during a storm, the can up right themselves or dig themselves out! They're semi-aggressive corals. The reproduce a-sexually by budding a small disc and eventually the females capture the sperm and fertilize the eggs internally. They develop and hatch out into the water calcium as ciliated larva. These larvae are pelagic for a time and then settle on the bottom and absorb their preferred species of zooxanthellae and grow and start their life on the sands! They prefer moderate to bright lights and slow to moderate water flow. Their temperature range should be 68 to 78 degrees. They seem to benefit from occasional zooplankton feedings.

Density 1.021 to 1.026	Silicate up to 0.05 ppm
Ph 7.9 to 8.2	Phosphate up to 0.005 ppm
Calcium 400.0 to 450.0 ppm	Nitrate up to 10.0 ppm
Magnesium 1100 to 1300 ppm	Nitrite 0.00 ppm
Stronium 7.0 to 10.0 ppm	Ammonia 0.00 ppm
Iron 0.1 to 0.3 ppm	Iodine 0.05 to 0.08 ppm

They seem to benefit from trace elements.

Chalice Corals (Echinophyllia Sp.)

These beautiful lps corals come in any different colors and combinations and are moderately easy to care for and prefer pristine water quality. They do well with sps corals. They prefer moderately lighting and moderate water flow. These encusting plating semi-aggressive corals have sweeper tentecles and need some space. They are slow growing and seem to benefit from occasional zooplankton feedings. Their temperature should be in the range of 68 to 78 degrees.

Density 1.021 to 1.026	Silicate up to 0.05 ppm
Ph 7.9 to 8.2	Phosphate up to 0.005 ppm
Calcium 400.0 to 450.0 ppm	Nitrate up to 10.0 ppm
Magnesium 1100 to 1300 ppm	Nitrite 0.00 ppm
Stronium 7.0 to 10.0 ppm	Ammonia 0.00 ppm
Iron 0.1 to 0.3 ppm	Iodine 0.05 to 0.08 ppm

They seem to benefit from trace elements.

Sps Corals

Small Polyp Stony Corals are the main group of reef building corals. They are fast growing and are what people think of when they want to see a coral reef. Most of these corals are tidal and grow in shallow seas. Sps Corals are easily broken during storms and frags are make in such a way. Many are hardy under the right conditions but are contankerus and demanding with the needs. They are one of the most beautiful groups of corals and colorful. They are worthy of ower effort.

Acropora Sp.

Reef building acropora corals grow a few different shapes plating, slender branched, and broad branching and come in a rainbow of colors and combinations of these colors. Acropora corals are the most demanding corals. They need pristine water quality and strong lighting! They have high calcium demands. They require rapid water movement in order to grow and prosper. The Acropora genus contains about 400 species. They are non-photosynthesizing and grow zooxanthellae in their tissue and receive most of their food energies this way. Sps corals are more sensitive to high temperatures and this can cause bleaching in the nano reef. Acropora grow moderately fast and can be cut back and fragged to start new colonies a-sexually. These trimmings will keep them to a desired shape in your nano reef. In the wild they also seasonally reproduce sexually. They are peaceful corals. Their temperature range should be 68 to 78 degrees.

Density 1.021 to 1.026	Silicate up to 0.00 ppm
Ph 7.9 to 8.2	Phosphate up to 0.00 ppm
Calcium 450.0 to 500.0 ppm	Nitrate up to 0.05 ppm
Magnesium 1200 to 1400 ppm	Nitrite 0.00 ppm
Stronium 8.0 to 10.0 ppm	Ammonia 0.00 ppm
Iron 0.1 to 0.3 ppm	Iodine 0.05 to 0.08 ppm

They seem to benefit from trace elements.

A. Millepora

These sps corals are moderate in their care but require rapid water flow and bright lighting. They grow moderately fast under proper conditions. They come in many colors; blue, red, purple and orange are some of the most common.

Tri-Color Acropora (A. Valida)

These sps corals have moderate care but require rapid water flow and bright lighting. They have thin branches and beautiful tri-colors like gold with deep purple tips and green polyps.w

Motipora

These reef bulding sps corals tend to do well in a nano reef. They refer strong water flow but their lighting can be less than Acropora sp. They are more hardy than some sps corals and more adaptive. There are at least 100 species and forms. They come in a rainbow of colors and combinations of these colors. Some are plating and have tiny polyps while others are encrusting and many are branching varieties. They're photosynthesizing and grow zooxanthellae in their tissue. They grow moderately fast under bright lighting and rapid water flow. They are usually sexual in the wild and a-sexual in the nano reef and they are easily trimmed to the desired look in your nano reef and fragged to make a new colony. They are peaceful corals. Their temperature should range from 68 to 78 degrees and are sensitive to high temperature. This may cause bleaching.

Density 1.021 to 1.026	Silicate up to 0.00 ppm
Ph 7.9 to 8.2	Phosphate up to 0.00 ppm
Calcium 400.0 to 450.0 ppm	Nitrate up to 0.05 ppm
Magnesium 1200 to 1400 ppm	Nitrite 0.00 ppm
Stronium 7.0 to 10.0 ppm	Ammonia 0.00 ppm
Iron 0.1 to 0.3 ppm	Iodine 0.05 to 0.08 ppm

They seem to benefit from trace elements.

Smooth Encrusting Montipora Coral (Montipora nodosa)

These sps corals have moderate care but require bright lighting and rapid water flow. These encrusting corals range in color from greens, purples and orange are the most common colors. They are a peaceful coral but are best grown on their own rock to reduce spreading. Their small polyps have a velvety look.

Montipora capricornis

These are a plating species, they do well in bright lighting and rapid water flow. These peaceful corals grow moderately fast and some of the most common colors are reds, purples and greens. They have very tiny polyps and thin plates that break easily so use caution. Because of this, they are best kept lower in the nano reef.

Montipora digitata

These branching sps corals are moderately easy to care for. They prefer bright lighting and rapid water flow. Some of their colors are greens, red, orange and purple. They are moderately fast growing. Their polyps have a fuzzy look when fully extended.

The Bird's Nest Coral (Seriatopora sp.)

These sps corals are moderately east to care for and are peaceful. They do well under bright lights and rapid water flow. They are often a pink or green color. The Birds Nest Coral has thin needle tipped branches and looks to size in a nano reef. They reproduce a-sexually in the nano and branches are easily broken and can be fragged to start a new colony. Their temperature should range from 68 to 78 degrees.

Density 1.021 to 1.026	Silicate up to 0.00 ppm
Ph 7.9 to 8.2	Phosphate up to 0.00 ppm
Calcium 400.0 to 450.0 ppm	Nitrate up to 0.05 ppm
Magnesium 1100 to 1300 ppm	Nitrite 0.00 ppm
Stronium 7.0 to 10.0 ppm	Ammonia 0.00 ppm
Iron 0.1 to 0.3 ppm	Iodine 0.05 to 0.08 ppm

They seem to benefit from trace elements.

Pocillopora damicornis

These are one of the easier sps corals. They do best under bright lights and rapid water flow. They usually are green or pink in color but do come in other colors. They are moderately peaceful corals. The water chemistry is the same as Seriatopora sp.

Cat's Paw Coral (Stylophora sp.)

These moderately easy corals do best under bright light and rapid watr flow. They're a pretty coral and have thick stocky branches. They are usually a pink or green color. Their water chemistry is the same as Seriatopora sp.

Turbinaria sp.

These are non-aggressive, easy sps corals. The genus of Turbinaria sp has 68 species and subspecies but only two species are commonly seen. The Cup Coral (Turbinaria peltata). They are from the Indio Pacific Ocean and the Red Sea. They are grey, green or brown in color. They range in different shapes, cup or wide mouth, coluims or ruffled edge looking. They are more adaptive then other species and do fine with moderate to bright lighting and moderate to rapid water flow. They have larger polyps. They seem to benefit from occasional zooplankton feedings.

The Scroll Coral (Turbinaria reniformis)

They usually are a yellowish, brown, grey or green color and some may have purple polyps or may be greenish in color and are pretty corals. Their shape ranges from flower looking to plates. They have smaller polyps and are thin and easily broken and fragged. They do well in moderate to bright lighting and moderate to rapid water flow. They may benefit from occasional zooplankton feedings.

Density 1.025 to 1.027	Temperature
Ph 8.2 to 8.4	Alkalinity 7 to 12 ppm
Calcium 400.0 to 450.0 ppm	Phosphate 0.00 ppm

Small Anemones (Order actiniaria)

Small anemones do well in the nano and there are many different species to choose from. Most large anemones are host to clown fish in the wild but most smaller anemones have commensal relationships with shrimp. These smaller anemones are adopted by clownfish in the nano reef so whatever you decide, shrimp or clownfish or both with your anemones. Clownfish are territorial and may force your shrimp out or kill them so if you do keep them together, more than one anemone will help this problem. Most anemones kept are photosynthesizing and grow coralline algae in their tissue but require feedings such as zooplankton, fish chunks, squid chunks or shrimp to eat. Many small anemones come in different colors and are beautiful. Caution, anemones can eat your fish or shrimp so choose their companions carefully!

Maxi-Mini Anemones (Stichodactyla topetum)

These small anemones grow up to 6 inches and are beautiful. They come in multi-color polyps and some of these are greens, yellows, oranges, reds, purples, pinks, whites, tans and browns. They are from the Indo-Pacific and beyond. They have at least two cousins, S. haddonii and S. gigantea. Maxi-mini anemones have a mild sting to other corals but can have a severe reaction to some people when handling them so use caution. They grow coralline algae in their tissue. They require moderate to bright lighting and moderate to rapid water flow. They are easy to care for and do well on the rock work. They're easy to frag and grow well. They should be fed daily or weekly depending on how much you feed them. They seem to benefit from Iodine trace elements. They usually reproduce a-sexually in the nano reef tank. They eat fish, shrimp, zooplankton and are easily fragged.

Flower Rock Sea Anemones (Phymanthus crucifer)

From: Florida and the Caribbean

Care: Easy to care for and prefer bright lights. They are photo-synthetic moderate water flow. They grow up to 32 feet deep in the wild!

Feeding: They require frequent feedings, mysis and shrimp work well

Reproduction: They reproduce frequently if fed well, a-sexually and sometimes shed sperm and eggs in the aquarium.

Size: They grow 5 or 6 inches and sometimes will have commensal relationships with clownfish in the reef tank but usually in the wild they are shrimp anemones and have a commensal relationships with them!

Color: They come in many different patterns and are every color of the rainbow and usually 2 or 3 colors per anemone.

Condy Anemones (Condylactis gigantea)

These anemones are from South Florida and the Caribbean. They grow up to 6 inches at the base and come in purples with green tips or pink with purple tips on the tentacles and greens, purples, pinks, tans, whites. The Condy Anemones are reef compatible but need some space and they can eat your fish and shrimp or crabs, so use caution! The toadfish (Opsanus sp.) and the red legged start eyed hermit crab (Dardanus venous) will eat them. They grow zooxanthellae in their tissue and are photosynthesizing anemones. They require moderate to bright lighting and moderate to rapid water flow. The Condy Anemones require daily or twice a week feedings of zooplankton, fish chunks, shrimp or squid. They seem to benefit from Iodine and trace elements. They reproduce usually a-sexually in the nano reef tank.

The Temperate Marine Nano Reef

There is many temperate marine life that can be kept with a chiller. These can be plants, corals, and starfish, hermit crabs, jellyfish and so on! Many species are difficult to acclimate to their nano reef tank. With some trial and error in this new hobby, this too can be perfected. There are many native marine species that can be collected with a fishing license and if a chiller is out of your price range, then a micro fridge can be converted by drilling on the sides or the top of the fridge and you can run rubber tubing through copper pipes or you can use

the fridge as a sump and place the sump inside with a inflow and outflow and seal the drilled holes with a pond foam after the pipes are in place. The nano tank will require at least ½ inch glass or plexi-glass with a cover to keep it cool and the thick glass helps reduce or alimanate condisation. This is fairly new to the hobby the temperate nano reef and with patients and time, we will perfect these reef tanks without a lid may be possible in a cool room!

Chapter 9

Cool Water Marine Fish

The Blue Banded Goby (Lythrypnus dalli)

Their neon reddish, orange and electric blue striped gobies are peaceful natured. They're from the Gulf of California to Northern Peru. They prefer rocky areas and will eat most foods offered. Their temperature should by 60 to 70 degrees.

The Blue Striped Jawfish (Opistognathus rosenblatti)

They have blue spots and are mouth brooders and are brownish. They prefer at least 6 inches of sand. Their temperature should be 60 to 70 degrees. They are from the Gulf of California. They are somewhat territorial and rocks should be used to divide and allow them to create territories. They eat most food offered.

Sticklebacks Aulorhynchidae

The family including sticklebacks. 16 species grouped into 5 genera and subspecies. They have tube snouts and are classified in the related family Aulo Hynchidae. Sticklebacks have no scales and some species have bony armor plated and are related to pipefish and seahorses. They are more commonly seen in the ocean but some are freshwater. Sticklebacks are carnivorous and eat crustaceans, insects and fish larvae. Most sticklebacks sexually mature at 2 inches and usually grow to 4 inches although the 15 spine stickleback (Spinachia spinachia) grow to 8.7 inches. Sticklebacks are nest builders out of plant matter. The male held together with a sticky secretion from the kidneys. The female lays her eggs in the nest and the male fertilize them and guards the eggs until they hatch.

The White-Spotted Strawberry Anemone (Urticina eques)

These corals are 4 inches but can grow to 6 inches and have smooth red column bases. They generally grow on rocky surfaces. They reproduce usually as the temperatures fall. The female lays large eggs up to 1,200 and are laid in intervals and males release sperm shortly thereafter. Some females have large oocytes and release eggs or gametes. The larva planula drift with the current. They feed on zooplankton and shrimp.

Orange Cup Coral (Balanophyllia elegans)

These corals have an iridescent shean algae and long clear tentacles. They are a true coral and down well in shaded areas of the nano and require regular plankton feedings. These lps corals have spirocyst which resemble nematocyst tentacles. They reproduce gastrovascular cavity and release into it and the eggs develop into planula and then are released into the water. They settle into tiny polyps and then secrete a skeleton.

Medridium senile

They have long thin cylindrical colim bases and are smooth. They have numerous short tentacles and are crownd looking divers color range and may have redish orange lips around their mouths. Their colors are white, cream, pink, orange, red, grey, brown and olive green with translucent tentacles and may have a white band. M. dianthus may have over a 1000 feathery tentacles. It can grow up to 12 inches tall but usually grows up to 6 inches high. M. senile is much smaller, around 1 inch with less than 200 tentacles. A dwarf race described as plankton feeders. They are hermaphrodites and the gonads can produce eggs or sperm and after one to six months, drifting in the plankton, they settle and metamorphosis into small anemones. They can a-sexually reproduce rapidly in the aquarium.

Aggregating Anemone (Anthropleura elegantissima)

These anemones are often found in rocky areas. They have zooxanthellae and are photosynthesizing. Size: 4 inches across and have around 100 tentacles most are olive green or bright green and some have pink tips. Reproduction sexually and a-sexually. They release gametes. They may proliferate through binary fission. They should be supplement fed with plankton.

Brooding Anemone (Epiactis prolifera)

These small green anemones. They all start life as a female but develop testes later in life, about ¾ inch and become hermaphrodites, self or cross fertilization. They can grow 2 inches but usually are 1 ¼ inches. They vary in color but usually are greenish brown but sometimes, red or green. They have fine white lines starting at the mouth and across the oral disc, the pedal disc can be blue on some anemones. They have 50 to 100 comical tentacles, each tipped with a terminal pore. The mother expels mucus and eggs out her mouth, they spread across her oral disc. Cilia move some down the column and attach to the base column. The larvae develop tentacles and live and grow protected by the mother for at least 3 months and separate around ¼ of an inch. They require regular feedings and eat plankton, fish, and shrimp. A predator the Leather Starfish (Dermasterias imbricata).

Sand Anemone (Phyllactis sp.)

These little anemones are sand dwellers and are borrowing. They grow about 3 inches but can grow to 6 inches.

Brown Cap Coral (Paracyathus stearnsii)

Probably non-photosynthesizing. A small solitary lps coral. This species is gonochoric and reproduce only sexually and are broadcast spawners. They may be bioluminescent.

Moon Jellyfish (Aurelia aurita)

They have four horseshoe gonads. The Moon jelly's are bell shaped. Their bodies are white in color and transparent. They have short tentacles with mild stinging affects. Moon Jellyfish typically grow two to six inches in diameter but up to 16 inches. They have a centralizing censoring system in their body that allows them to find prey. They have no brain and are made up of 95% water. The Moon jellyfish will do well in a 15 to 20 gallon kreisel nano tank with a soft current they will rotate gently. They do best with a temperature around 50 to 70 degrees. They will eat plankton. Reproduction: Shedding eggs and sperm on a daily basis and a-sexual reproduction is more likely in the aquarium. The young polyps may be striped or have spots in the middle of the bell. Jellyfish are cnidarians which means corals and anemones and hydroids are their closest living relatives. They generally reach sexual maturity around 3 months of age. They have short tentacles with nematocysts but their stings are very mild. They can survive in brackish seawater but do best in full marine seawater. Their polyps typically grow in the bottom of the tank and bud into a four stage polyps or medusa and are released into free swimming jellyfish. They typically live 6 months to a year. There are many species of jellyfish to choose from that make great nano tank companions.

Chapter 10 Coral Reef Ponds for Indoor, Outdoor or the Greenhouse

Coral reef ponds are new to the hobby but can be very beautiful in the home or sunroom or greenhouse and if you live in a mild climate area under protection from the weather with proper heating and cooling with larger chillers outdoor glass front coral reef ponds are possible! You can make a circular pond for moon jellyfish with Led color changing lights or other jellyfish species like the upside down Jellyfish (Cassiopea sp.). Some species of turtles can be kept in the coral pond like the diamond back terrapes (Malaclemys terrapin) with minimum damage to the reef. Pond foam can be cut or shaped with forms like plastic wire or pvc pipe frames around and in the pond. Non-toxic and water proof paints and colored sand can be added and held in place with non-toxic waterproof spray glue or silicone and seashells pond foam also acts as an insulator.

Concrete Ponds

Concrete ponds can be shaped into form with plastic wire and pvc pipe frames and color sand. Large and small seashells can be added to the concrete mix. The concrete mix should be on the dry side and added to the forms inside and outside of the pond. Plant holders can be added to the concrete forms.

Glass or Plexi-Glass Front Ponds

There are three ways to make a glass front nano or large pond.

1. You can use plastic containers, 20-gallons or more or plastic pond liners or plastic stock tanks. You can measure and then cut with a power saw. Cut a larger hole in the side of the container, cut and bend the plexi-glass, roll it and tie it then put it in the oven for 10 minutes at 140 to 160 degrees. Then put the plex-glass into place and use a heavy amount of silicone sealant and maybe plastic nuts and bolts to clamp it in place. Fill with water and test for leaks and drain and seal all leaks and let sit for 24 hours more. Rinse pond and decorate inside and

out to your desire with pond foam that looks like rocks or bamboo or reed, strip branches, whatever you can think of for your coral reef pond!

2. Glass ponds can be made like an aquarium but needs to be at least 40-gallons or more. A triangle style is nice or squared shape panels whatever design you can come up with. The glass panels should be at least a half inch thick, the sides and back can be pond foamed, inside and out to look like rocks or whatever style you desire.

3. Concrete and cylinder block coral ponds cylinder blocks can be shaped in a triangle with a glass front or a half moon circle with a glass front or any shape you desire. Then concrete with plastic wire and pvc pipe frames you can shape rocks around the sides or in the pond with live plants and pot planters in the rock forms. Cylinder blocks and concrete ponds are generally shaded. Outdoor ponds in a house under lights or in a sun room or in a greenhouse all are good places but outdoor ponds for coral reefs are more difficult but not impossible.

Chapter 11   Coral Medical Uses

Corals have many medical uses and have proven beneficial to mankind's health and different species may prove to have other medical uses so sustaining are reefs and captive coral population may help to advance medical science.

Beta 2- Adrenergic Agonist

The Beta 2 adrenergic agonist effects the muscles to relax, dilation of the bronchial passages, vasodilation in muscles and liver, relax the uterine muscle and the release of insulin.

Side Effects: Insomnia, anxiety, tremors occur in some patients and increased heart rate.

Salmeterol

Salmeterol in a long lasting beta2 adrenergic receptor agonist drug used in maintaining and preventing asthma symptoms and chronic obstructive pulmonary disease or COPD and these symptoms may be shortness of breath, wheezing, coughing and chest tightness and breathing difficulties and bronchospasm during exercise. Salmeterol last up 5.5 to 12 hours.

Side Effects: Dizziness, sinus infection and migraine headaches. These are usually minor.

Formoterol

Formoterol is a long lasting beta2 adrenergic agonist used for asthma and chronic obstructive pulmonary disease also known as COPD. Formoterol is faster acting than salmeterol the result of lower lipophilicity and has been known to be more effective. A 12mg dose of formoterol is the same as a 50mg dose of Salmeterol. Formoterol lasts up to 10-12 hours. Possible use for obesity, it increases energy utilization, fat metabolism.

Side affects: Activation of B type 1 receptors resulting in excessive increases of the heart rate.

Formoterol may also be useful in the treatment of down syndrome by strengthening the nerve connections in the hippocampus, the brain center used for spatial navigation, paying attention and forming new memories.

Formoterol may also stimulate mitochondrial biogenesis mitochondrial dysfunction like degenerative diseases, particularly neurogenerative disorders.

Antineoplastic

The Antineoplastic are inhibiting, maturation and proliferation of malignant cells a chemotherapeutic agent that controls or kills cancer cells. Most anticancer drugs prevent the proliferation of cells by inhibiting the synthesis of deoxyribonucleic acid or DNA. Anticancer drugs interfere with DNA replication by causing cross-linking DNA strands and abnormal pairing of nucleotides.

Estramustine

Estramustine is an anti-microtubule chemotherapy agent used to treat prostate cancer. The therapeutic actions are believed to be related to its ability to depolymerizing the microtubules by binding microtubule with associated proteins and this arrest prostate cancer cells. There are many side effects that are possible but are rare 1 to 10%.

Flutamide

Flutamide is a non-steroidal antiandrogen used primarily to treat prostate cancer by bonding to the prostate glands. It has also been used in hyperandrogenism or excessive androgen levels in woman like polycystic ovary syndrome also known as PCOS and hirsutism. Flutamide has also been used as a hormone replacement therapy for transsexual woman. Flutamide has a fairly short half life about 5 to 6 hours in the body.

Danazol

Danazol is a derivative of the synthetic steroid ethisterone. Danazol prevents ovulation by suppressing the increase of luteinizing hormone during the menstrual cycle and helps inhibit ovarian steroidogenesis which may decrease secretion of estradiol. This may increase the androgen. It displaces testosterone from sex hormone-binding globulin (SHBG) and displacing it and increasing serum testosterone levels. Danazol directly stimulates androgens and progesterone receptors. It's also used in treating menorrhagia, fibrocystic breast disease, immune thrombocytopenic purpura, premenstrual syndrome, breast pain investigated in treating diabetic macular edema. Danazol has many side effects but has proven to be helpful. Danazol lasts 3 to 6 hours from a single dose.

Exemestane

Exemestane is used in the treatment of breast-cancer and post menopause in women. This class of drug is called "aromatase" inhibitor. What this enzyme does is synthesis of estrogen so this lowers estrogen levels and slows the growth of cancers. Exemistone is irreversible steroidal aromatase in activator. It permanently binds to enzymes preventing them from converting androgen into estrogen. Exemestane also acts as a suicide inhibitor.

Corticosteroids

Corticosteroids are a class of chemicals that produce adrenal cortex and synthesize analogous of these hormones. Corticosteroids are helpful with stress and immune response. They are beneficial in regulating inflammation. Carbohydrate metabolism, protein catabolism, blood electrolyte levels and behavior. Corticosteroids are used for a range of conditions from brain tumors to skin diseases.

Budesonide

Budesonide is a gluecarticoid steroid used for the treatment of asthma, COPD and other allergies. The treatment of bowel disease and this includes Chron's Disease and ulcerate colitis. Budesonide has a biological half life of 2.0 to 3.6 hours.

Fluticasone propionate

Fluticasone propionate is a corticosteroids called glucocorticoids are hormones that predominately affect the metabolism of carbohydrates to a lesser extent fat and protein. It helps to treat asthma, allergic rhinitis, nasal polyps, many different skin disorders and Crohn's Disease. Ulcerative Colitis and eosinophilic oesophagitis. It is highly selective against at the glucocorticoids receptor with negligible activity at androgen, estrogen, mineralocorticoid receptors, producing anti-inflammatory and vasoconstriction effects. It has a topical effect on the lungs, fluticasone propionate has also showed to have benefits with celiac disease. Fluticasone propionate in combination with other drugs helps treat HIV and antifungal drug. It has a biological half life of 10 hours.

Fluticasone Furoate

Fluticasone Furoate is used for allergies particularly rhinitis including chronic bronchitis and emphysema. Mainly for long term treatment airflow obstruction and COPD.

Mometasone Furoate

Mometasone Furoate is a glucocorticosteroid it's used in the treatment of skin disorders like Eczema and Psoriasis, Rhinitis or Hay Fever for severe asthma that are less responsive to high dose of corticosteroids and penile phimosis. It's also used for asthma with formoterol due to its anti-inflammatory properties to the lungs. Mometasone Furoate Is a stronger steroid than hydrocortisone and dexamethasone is more potent. It may help treat adenoids hypertrophy in children. Mometasone furoate can reverse activating inflammatory proteins, reestablishing cell membranes and decreasing influx of inflammatory cells. Mometasone furoate is very potent against invarious types of cells like mastocytes and eosinophils and helps circulate the blood like other corticosteroids. Mometasone furoate monohydrate is used mostly for asthma and other disorders. Mometasone furoate has a biological half life of 5.8 hours.

Isoflupredone Acetate

This corticosteroid is an anti-inflammatory and is used for cattle, horses, pigs and other farm life. Isoflupredone Acetate is used for severe infection and toxicity. Like milk fever, shock, infection, dystocia, retained placenta, bovine, ketosis, muscular skeletal conditions allergic reactions inflammatory ocular-conditions and other treatments.

Hormones

Hormones are used for organs, tissue functions lungs sensory perception, stress, reproduction, growth and development and mood and other functions. Hormones target specific cells in the body by binding a specific receptor proteins and can change in cell functions.

Norethisterone

Norethitherone is used as a female hormone treatment like menstral cycles painful or heavy periods or conditions called endometriosis. This is caused by tissue normally found in the womb and this tissure becomes trapped in other parts of the body, often in the pelvic area. This is what causes heavy or painful periods. Norethitherone is also used in the treatment of some female cancer like breast cancer.

Antihistamines

Antihistamines are used to suppress or opposite the activity of histamine receptors in the body. Antihistamines mainly used for allergies, insomnia and sometimes used for vertigo like inner ear infections, gastric acid, peptic ulcers and acid reflux.

Azelastine hydrochloride

Azelastine hydrochloride is used for seasonal allergies, rhinitis such as runny nose, sneezing. This antihistamine blocks histamines caused by allergic symptoms. Azelastine hydrochloride has half like of 22 hours.

Coral Bone Graft Substitute

Corals are now being used in bone grafting in the human body. Their porous structure makes them ideal for tissue and bone growth. The corals calcium-carbonate is what is used for bone grafting. This is called coralline hydroxyapatite calcium carbonate. This allows for the coral graft to dissolve away and the bone will fuse together without growing bacteria in the bone fuse. Coral bone grafts may soon be used more extensively.